G. SCHIRMER'S COLLECTION OF OPERA LIBRETTOS

FALSTAFF

Lyric Comedy in Three Acts

Based on Shakespeare's "The Merry Wives of Windsor"
and passages from "Henry IV"

Music by

Giuseppe Verdi

Libretto by
ARRIGO BOITO

English Version by
WALTER DUCLOUX

Ed. 2519

G. SCHIRMER, *Inc.*

DISTRIBUTED BY

HAL•LEONARD®
CORPORATION
7777 W. BLUEMOUND RD. P.O. BOX 13819 MILWAUKEE, WI 53213

Important Notice

Performances of this opera must be licensed by the publisher.

All rights of any kind with respect to this opera and any parts thereof, including but not limited to stage, radio, television, motion picture, mechanical reproduction, translation, printing, and selling are strictly reserved.

License to perform this work, in whole or in part, whether with instrumental or keyboard accompaniment, must be secured in writing from the Publisher. Terms will be quoted upon request.

Copying of either separate parts or the whole of this work, by hand or by any other process, is unlawful and punishable under the provisions of the U.S.A. Copyright Act.

The use of any copies, including arrangements and orchestrations, other than those issued by the Publisher, is forbidden.

All inquiries should be directed to the Publisher:

G. Schirmer Rental Department
5 Bellvale Road
Chester, NY 10918
(914) 469-2271

FALSTAFF

"He is a man at once young and old, enterprising and fat, a dupe and a wit, harmless and wicked, weak in principle and resolute by constitution, cowardly in appearance and brave in reality, a knave without malice, a liar without deceit, and a knight, a gentleman, and a soldier, without either dignity, decency, or honor. No ridicule can destroy him; he is safe even in defeat and seems to rise, like another Antaeus, with recruited vigor at every fall."

MAURICE MORGANN

Giuseppe Verdi (1813-1901) was born into a period when Italian comic opera, after more than a century of world-wide triumph, was losing its appeal. The failure of his first work, an *opera buffa* called *Un Giorno di Regno (King for a Day)* no doubt helped to guide the young composer in the direction of musical tragedy, and it was there that Verdi achieved his towering stature. In *Otello,* premiered when he was 73 years old, he set himself a monument which is likely to stand for a long time as an unsurpassed masterpiece in the field of musical tragedy.

Yet, as *opera buffa* receded into the past, Verdi realized more and more that opera needs laughter as well as tears. The time-honored symbol of the stage does show one weeping and one laughing mask. Shakespeare, Verdi's idol as a playwright — he called him "papa" — was equally at home in tragedy and in comedy. Times had, of course, changed, and Italian opera could not return to the pratfalls and guffaws of a hundred years ago. But it was time someone re-introduced the smile onto the operatic stage, and who could do that better than that incredible combination of farmer, patriot, businessman, benefactor, and genius called Giuseppe Verdi?

The bulky figure of Sir John Falstaff had occupied Verdi for many years. But other tasks took precedence, and it was not until 1889 that Arrigo Boito, encouraged by the composer, sent the latter a draft of a libretto which immediately won Verdi's approval. Boito, a man of brilliant endowments both as a musician and a man of letters, had already written the libretto to *Otello* and knew what Verdi wanted. Their *Falstaff* is actually an amalgam of the two Shakespearean characters, the finely drawn figure from *King Henry IV* and the sorry caricature of knightliness gone to seed from *The Merry Wives of Windsor.* The plot is that of the latter comedy.

Yet, the Maestro was 76 years old. World-famous, rich, and wise, should he not leave well enough alone? Would he live long enough to finish a task which could not be tossed off in a few months but would take years to complete? With remarkable insight, Boito allayed the old man's fears with a simple statement: "There is only one way to end your life's work more fittingly than with *Otello.* That is to end it with *Falstaff.*"

First produced at La Scala on February 9, 1893, *Falstaff* was an immediate success. The title-role was sung by Victor Maurel who also played the part in the first performance in North America, at the Metropolitan Opera House on February 4, 1895. Another notable Metropolitan production occurred in 1909, with Toscanini conducting a brilliant cast headed by Antonio Scotti and Emmy Destinn. Scotti sang the part again in 1925, this time opposite Lucrezia Bori, Beniamino Gigli, and Frances Alda. The part of Ford was entrusted to a newcomer who became an overnight sensation and subsequently was to carry the prestige of the American singer to new heights: Lawrence Tibbett. Since then, Falstaff has won an ever-increasing audience all over America.

W. D.

THE STORY

ACT I. *Part 1.* John Falstaff, once a companion of kings but now little more than a bulky wreck of his former self, is putting the finishing touches to two letters, undisturbed by the anger of Dr. Cajus who berates him for allowing his two henchmen, Bardolph and Pistol, to rob him. Grandly dismissing the doctor, Falstaff tells his two companions of his sly scheme: The letters are to be sent to two young matrons of Windsor, Alice Ford and Meg Page. Both their beauty and their husbands' wealth have caught Sir John's fancy. When the two cronies refuse to act as letter-bearers, stating that such a service would be incompatible with their honor, Falstaff hands the letters to a page. He furiously turns on his henchmen, ridiculing their recourse to honor and claiming honor to be no more than a figment of illusion. Grabbing a broom, he chases the two from the "Garter Inn."

Part 2. Mrs. Ford and Mrs. Page, meeting in front of Ford's house, compare the two identical letters they have just received and resolve to punish the old Lothario for his duplicity. Bardolph and Pistol have come to Mr. Ford to warn him of Falstaff's designs on his wife. They are joined by Dr. Cajus and young Fenton who are rivals for the hand of Ford's daughter, Ann. While Ann loves Fenton, her father favors Cajus as a son-in-law. Ford, insanely jealous, makes plans to investigate the relationship between his wife and Sir John by visiting the latter under an assumed name. The women in turn decide to dispatch Dame Quickly to the Inn. She is to invite Falstaff to a tender appointment with Mrs. Ford while her husband is absent.

ACT II. *Part 1.* A little while later, the two cronies, asking Falstaff's pardon, rejoin him at the Inn. After a ceremonious greeting, Dame Quickly assures the Fat Knight of the infatuation of his two "conquests," inviting him to visit Mrs. Ford between two and three in the afternoon. Accepting the tender summons, Falstaff credits his imposing appearance with his irresistible appeal to women. Equipped with attractive credentials, a jug of Cyprus wine and a bag of gold, Ford enters, introducing himself as "Mr. Brook." He pretends to be madly in love with Mrs. Ford and enlists Falstaff's help in breaking her resistance to his advances. Sir John takes "Mr. Brook" into his confidence and tells him of the forthcoming tryst. Left alone, Ford erupts in a wild denunciation of woman's infidelity and praises his own jealousy for having warned him of the impending disaster. Dressed in his best finery, Falstaff, escorted by "Mr. Brook," leaves the Inn for the Ford home.

Part 2. The merry wives of Windsor prepare for Falstaff's visit. While they arrange the living-room, Alice Ford assures her daughter of her help in warding off Dr. Cajus as a candidate for Ann's hand. — With courtly flourish Falstaff greets his *adorata* who coyly evades his advances. Their tête-à-tête is interrupted by the arrival of Meg while Sir John hides behind a screen. According to plan, Meg paints a fearsome picture of Ford approaching in a wild fury. The fib, however, turns out to be reality: Ford is indeed "rolling in like thunder" amidst a group of neighbors. Together with Bardolph, Pistol, and Cajus they search the house for the culprit. Ford's suspicion is aroused by a huge clothes-basket whose contents he scatters without finding his prey. While the men are out of the room, the women hide Falstaff in the basket. Ann and Fenton, oblivious of their surroundings, kiss each other behind the screen. At the sound of the kiss, the hunters think they have found their quarry. When they discover their error, Alice has the basket emptied out of the window into the Thames. Ford and the others arrive just in time to witness Falstaff's humiliation, and their fury dissolves in general hilarity.

v

ACT III. *Part 1*. Wrapped in blankets outside the "Garter Inn" while his clothes are drying on the line, Falstaff is in a somber mood. A jug of hot sack revives his spirits when Quickly brings him a letter from Mrs. Ford. Soon enough, his initial indignation yields to a new spirit of adventure and he agrees to follow the instructions contained in the letter: To appear at the stroke of midnight at the legendary Oak of Herne deep in Windsor Forest, disguised as the "Black Hunter" and wearing a pair of antlers. He invites Quickly to join him inside the Inn. This time, all his enemies have joined in the plan to punish the old rogue once and for all. While the Fords, Meg, Ann, and Fenton attend to the final details, Cajus wins Ford's consent to marry Ann that night. Quickly overhears their secretive conversation and decides to help Ann escape a fate worse than death.

Part 2. Near the Oak of Herne, the preparations for Falstaff's undoing are almost completed. Fenton awaits his beloved, but her mother gives him instructions which will help her thwart her husband's scheme. — Falstaff appears just as midnight sounds from the distant belfry. In the moonlit night, he is joined by Alice. Within a few moments, however, she is driven away by the approach of an unholy host of elfins, goblins, and other ghostly creatures. They discover Falstaff hiding near the Oak and visit merciless punishment on the human intruder by rolling and pinching him. Suddenly, the hood slips off one of his tormentors and discloses Bardolph. Now aware of the nature of his foes, Falstaff breaks out in a burst of fury. Alone against everyone else, he proudly takes credit for having brought some mirth into the pedestrian lives of his fellow-men of Windsor. The ridicule at first directed against Falstaff soon finds a new target: Ford. Due to the wily women, his plan of uniting Cajus and Ann has gone sadly astray. After Ford has given his blessing to two veiled couples, one of them turns out to be Ann and Fenton and the other . . . Bardolph and Dr. Cajus, whose "wedding" provokes gales of laughter. Back in everyone's good grace, Falstaff leads the merry assembly in a rousing tribute to folly as the true spice of life that makes man what he is.

CAST OF CHARACTERS

SIR JOHN FALSTAFF . . . . Baritone

FENTON, a young gentleman . . . . Tenor

FORD, a wealthy burgher . . . . Baritone

Dr. CAJUS, a physician . . . . Tenor

BARDOLPH ⎱
⎰ followers of Falstaff . . . . Tenor

PISTOL . . . . Bass

MRS. ALICE FORD . . . . Soprano

ANNE (Nannetta), her daughter . . . . Soprano

MRS. MEG PAGE . . . . Mezzo-Soprano

DAME QUICKLY . . . . Mezzo-Soprano

ROBIN, Falstaff's page

An Innkeeper in Ford's household

Burghers and street-folk; Ford's servants; Maskers as elves, fairies, witches; etc.

PLACE: Windsor

TIME: Reign of King Henry IV

SYNOPSIS OF SCENES

FALSTAFF

ATTO PRIMO

Parte Prima

L'interno dell'Osteria dell Giarrettiera. Una tavola. Un gran seggiolone. Una panca. Sulla tavola i resti d'un desinare, parecchie bottiglie e un bicchiere. Calamaio, penne, carta, una candela accesa. Una scopa appoggiata al muro. Uscio nel fondo, porta a sinistra.

Falstaff è occupato a riscaldare la cera di due lettere alla fiamma della candela, poi le suggella con un anello. Dopo averle suggellate, spegne il lume e si mette a bere comodamente sdraiato sul seggiolone.

Falstaff, Dr. Cajus, Bardolfo, Pistola, l'oste nel fondo.

DR. CAJUS
(entrando dalla porta a sinistra e gridando minaccioso)
Falstaff!

FALSTAFF
(senz' abbadare alle vociferazioni del Dr. Cajus, chiama l'oste che si avvicina)
Olà!

DR. CAJUS
(più f....e di prima)
Sir John Falstaff!

BARDOLFO *(al Dr. Cajus)*
Oh! che vi piglia?

DR. CAJUS
(sempre vociando e avvicinandosi a Falstaff, che non gli dà retta)
Hai battuto i miei servi!
Sforzata la mia casa.

FALSTAFF *(all'oste)*
Oste! un'altra bottiglia di Xeres.

DR. CAJUS
Hai fiaccata la mia giumenta baia,

FALSTAFF
Ma non la tua massaia.

DR. CAJUS
Troppa grazia! Una vecchia cisposa.
Ampio Messere, se foste venti
Volte John Falstaff Cavaliere
Vi forzerò a rispondermi.

FALSTAFF *(con flemma)*
Ecco la mia risposta:
Ho fatto ciò che hai detto.

DR. CAJUS
E poi?

FALSTAFF
. . . l'ho fatto apposta.

DR. CAJUS *(gridando)*
M'appellerò al Consiglio Real.

FALSTAFF
Vatti con Dio. Sta zitto o avrai le beffe;
Quest'è il consiglio mio.

DR. CAJUS
(ripigliando la sfuriata contro Bardolfo)
Non è finita!!

FALSTAFF
Al diavolo!

DR. CAJUS
Bardolfo!

BARDOLFO
Ser Dottore.

DR. CAJUS
Tu, ier, m'hai fatto bere.

BARDOLFO
Pur troppo! e che dolore!
(Si fa tastare il polso dal Dr. Cajus)
Sto mal. D'un tuo pronostico m'assisti.
Ho l'intestino guasto. Malanno agl'osti
Che dan la calce al vino!
(mettendo l'indice sul proprio naso enorme)
Vedi questa meteora?

DR. CAJUS
La vedo.

BARDOLFO
Essa si corca rossa così ogni notte.

1

FALSTAFF

ACT ONE

PART ONE

Inside the Garter Inn.

A table. A large armchair. A bench. On the table the remnants of a meal, several bottles, and a goblet. An inkwell with quills, some paper and a lit candle. A broom leaning against the wall. A main entrance upstage, another door to the left.

Falstaff is busy heating a stick of sealing-wax over the candle and sealing two letters with the help of a ring. This done, he extinguishes the candle and starts drinking, stretched out comfortably in the armchair.

Falstaff, Dr. Cajus, Bardolph, Pistol. The innkeeper in the background.

DR. CAJUS
(entering from door at left, shouting menacingly)
Falstaff!

FALSTAFF
(ignoring him, calls the innkeeper who moves closer)
Come here!

DR. CAJUS
(raising his voice even more)
Sir John Falstaff!

BARDOLPH *(to Dr. Cajus)*
Oh! Why the shouting?

DR. CAJUS
(still shouting and approaching Falstaff who pays no attention to him)
You've mistreated my servants! . . .

FALSTAFF
(to the innkeeper)
Quickly! Go! Bring me some more of this sherry!

DR. CAJUS
You have beaten my mare until she's dying, you broke into my quarters.

FALSTAFF
But spared your keeper's crying!

DR. CAJUS
Thank you kindly! Such an ugly old creature!
Mighty Sir Mountain, if twenty times as noble and twenty times Sir Falstaff
I'd force you yet to answer me.

FALSTAFF *(lazily)*
Well then, I'll tell you loudly:
I've done the things you mention . . .

DR. CAJUS
Go on!

FALSTAFF
. . . and done them proudly.

DR. CAJUS *(screaming)*
I shall appeal to the Court of the King.

FALSTAFF
Heaven may keep you! The joke will be on you, Sir.
Take it from me, John Falstaff!

DR. CAJUS
(turning his fury on Bardolph)
And now to this one!

FALSTAFF
To hell with you!

DR. CAJUS
You rascal!

BARDOLPH
Honored doctor!

DR. CAJUS
Last night we both were drinking.

BARDOLPH
Indeed, Sir! I still am paying the bill!
(inviting Cajus to feel his pulse)
I need your help, my dear physician.
Have I a shrunken liver? This blasted host must have thinned his wine with poison!
(pointing to his own nose)
See what shines here so brightly!

DR. CAJUS
I see it.

BARDOLPH
Fiery and red, it glows like a star in the darkness.

DR. CAJUS (*scoppiando*)
Pronostico di forca!
M'hai fatto ber, furfante, con lui
　　　(*indicando Pistola*)
Narrando frasche;
Poi, quando fui ben ciùschero,
M'hai vuotate le tasche.

BARDOLFO (*con decoro*)
Non io.
　　　　　DR. CAJUS
Chi fu?

FALSTAFF (*chiamando Pistola*)
Pistola!
　　　　PISTOLA (*avanzandosi*)
Padrone.
　　　　　FALSTAFF
(*sempre seduto sul seggiolone e con
　flemma*)
Hai tu vuotate le tasche a quel
　Messere?
　　　　　DR. CAJUS
　　　(*scattando contro Pistola*)
Certo fu lui. Guardate
　come s'atteggia al niego
Quel ceffo da bugiardo!
　　　(*vuotando una tasca del farsetto*)
Qui c'eran due scellini del regno
　d'Edoardo
E sei mezze-corone.
Non ne riman più segno.

PISTOLA
(*dignitosamente brandendo la scopa*)
Padron, chiedo di battermi con quest'
　arma di legno.
　　　(*al Dr. Cajus, con forza*)
Vi smentisco!
　　　　DR. CAJUS
Bifolco! tu parli a un gentiluomo!

　　　　　PISTOLA
Gonzo!
　　　　　DR. CAJUS
Pezzente!
　　　　　PISTOLA
Bestia!
　　　　　DR. CAJUS
Can!
　　　　　PISTOLA
Vil!
　　　　　DR. CAJUS
Spauracchio!
　　　　　PISTOLA
Gnomo!

DR. CAJUS
Germoglio di mandràgora!

PISTOLA
Chi?
　　　　DR. CAJUS
Tu.
　　　　PISTOLA
Ripeti!
　　　　DR. CAJUS
Sì.
　　　　PISTOLA
(*scagliandosi contro il Dr. Cajus*)
Saete!!!
　　　　FALSTAFF
(*Al cenno di Falstaff, Pistola si frena.*)
Ehi là! Pistola! Non scaricarti qui.
　　　(*chiamando Bardolfo*)
Bardolfo! Chi ha vuotate le tasche a
　quel Messere?

DR. CAJUS (*subito*)
Fu l'un dei due.

BARDOLFO
(*con serenità, indicando il Dr. Cajus*)
Costui beve, poi pel gran bere
Perde i suoi cinque sensi,
Poi ti narra una favola
Ch'egli ha sognato mentre dormì sotto
　la tavola.

FALSTAFF (*al Dr. Cajus*)
L'odi? Se ti capaciti, del ver tu sei
　sicuro.
I fatti son negati. Vattene in pace.

DR. CAJUS
Giuro che se mai mi ubbriaco ancora
　all'osteria
Sarà fra gente onesta,
Sobria, civile e pia.

　　　(*Esce dalla porta a sinistra.*)

BARDOLFO, PISTOLA
(*accompagnando buffonescamente sino
　all'uscio il Dr. Cajus e salmodiando*)
Amen!
　　　　FALSTAFF
Cessi l'antifona. La urlate in contrat-
　tempo.
(*Bardolfo e Pistola smettono e si avvici-
　nano a Falstaff.*)
L'arte sta in questa massima:
Rubar con garbo e a tempo

DR. CAJUS (*furious*)
A light by which to hang you!
You made me drunk, you rascal,
(*pointing to Pistol*)
while he was telling stories.
Then, when my mind was deaf and
numb, you took all I had on me.

BARDOLPH (*with dignity*)
Not I!

DR. CAJUS
Who then?

FALSTAFF (*addressing Pistol*)
You, Pistol!

PISTOL (*approaching Falstaff*)
My master?

FALSTAFF
(*still stretching lazily in his chair*)
Have you divested this man of his be-
longings?

DR. CAJUS
(*advancing on Pistol*)
Yes, it was he! Behold him!
Read what his snout is telling although
he would deny it!
(*turning his pockets inside out*)
I know that I had on me two good Ed-
wardian shillings and six florins of
silver.
Nothing is left, so help me!

PISTOL
(*solemnly brandishing the broom*)
Sir John, allow me kindly now to sweep
him off the premises!
(*to Dr. Cajus, with intent*)
You're a liar!

DR. CAJUS
You blockhead! Offend a man of station!

PISTOL
Stupid!

DR. CAJUS
You beggar!

PISTOL
Varlet!

DR. CAJUS
Dog!

PISTOL
Lout!

DR. CAJUS
You scarecrow!

PISTOL
Pixy!

DR. CAJUS
You feeble-minded idiot!

PISTOL
Who?

DR. CAJUS
You!

PISTOL
You mean it?

DR. CAJUS
Yes.

PISTOL
(*attacking Dr. Cajus*)
I'll show you!

FALSTAFF
(*motioning Pistol to hold back*)
Wait! Wait! You hothead! This is no
place to fight.
(*to Bardolph*)
You, Bardolph ... who has emptied the
pockets of the doctor?

DR. CAJUS (*quickly*)
I'm sure they both did!

BARDOLPH
(*serenely pointing to Dr. Cajus*)
He was drinking, heavily drinking,
Till he had lost his senses.
Now he tells you a fairy-tale, some
fancy fable
No doubt dreamed up while under the
table.

FALSTAFF (*to Dr. Cajus*)
Well now ... this man's veracity can
not in faith be doubted.
Your statements stand refuted. I bid
you leave in peace.

DR. CAJUS
Hear me! If I drink once again and
lower my defences
'Twill be with men of worth and honor
who pay their expenses!
(*Exits through the door at the left.*)

BARDOLPH, PISTOL
(*escorting the Doctor to the door, grotesquely chanting*)
Amen!

FALSTAFF
Cease your antiphonals! Your counter-
point is dreadful.
(*Bardolph and Pistol stop singing and
draw nearer to Falstaff.*)
Theft has its laws of artistry:
To steal with charm and good timing!

Siete dei rozzi artisti.

(*Si mette ad esaminare il conto che l'oste avrà portato insieme alla bottiglia di Xeres.*)

6 polli: 6 scellini. 30 giarre di Xeres:
2 lire, 3 tacchini.

(*a Bardolfo, gettandogli la borsa, e si rimette a leggere lentamente:*)

Fruga nella mia borsa.
2 fagiani. Un'acciuga.

BARDOLFO

(*Estrae dalla borsa le monete e le conta sul tavolo.*)

Un mark, un mark, un penny.

FALSTAFF

Fruga.

BARDOLFO

Ho frugato.

FALSTAFF

Fruga!

BARDOLFO

(*gettando la borsa sul tavolo*)

Qui non c'è più uno spicciolo.

FALSTAFF (*alzandosi*)

Sei la mia distruzione!
Spendo ogni sette giorni dieci ghinee!
Beone!
So che se andiam, la notte, di taverna
in taverna,
Quel tuo naso ardentissimo mi serve da
lanterna!
Ma quel risparmio d'olio tu lo consumi
in vino.
Son trent'anni che abbevero
Quel fungo porporino!
Costi troppo.

(*a Pistola, poi all'oste*)

E tu pure. Oste! un'altra bottiglia.

(*a Bardolfo e Pistola*)

Mi struggete le carni! Se Falstaff
s'assottiglia
Non è più lui, nessun più l'ama; in
quest'addome
C'è un migliaio di lingue che annunci-
ano il mio nome!

PISTOLA (*acclamando*)

Falstaff immenso!

BARDOLFO

Enorme Falstaff!

FALSTAFF

(*guardandosi e toccandosi l'addome*)

Quest'è il mio regno. Lo ingrandirò.
Ma è tempo d'assottigliar l'ingegno.

BARDOLFO, PISTOLA

Assottigliam.

(*tutti e tre in crocchio*)

FALSTAFF

V'è noto un tal, qui del paese che ha
nome Ford?

BARDOLFO

Sì.

PISTOLA

Sì.

FALSTAFF

Quell'uomo è un gran borghese.

PISTOLA

Più liberal d'un Creso.

BARDOLFO

E' un Lord!

FALSTAFF

Sua moglie è bella.

PISTOLA

E tien lo scrigno.

FALSTAFF

È quella! O amor! Sguardo di stella!
Collo di cigno! e il labbro? un fior. Un
fior che ride.
Alice è il nome, e un giorno come passar mi vide
Ne' suoi paraggi, rise. M'ardea l'estro
amatorio
Nel cor. La Dea vibrava raggi di spec-
chio ustorio

(*pavoneggiandosi*)

Su me, su me, sul fianco baldo, sul gran
torace,
Sul maschio pie', sul fusto saldo, erto,
capace;
E il suo desir in lei fulgea sì al mio
congiunto
Che parea dir: «Io son di Sir John
Falstaff»

BARDOLFO

Punto.

FALSTAFF

E a capo. Un'altra;

Ludicrous pair of artists!

(*He starts examining the bill which the innkeeper has brought along with the bottle of sherry.*)

Six pullets: six shillings. Thirty flagons of sherry:

Two florins. Three partridges . . .

(*to Bardolph, throwing him his purse, then slowly reading on*)

See how much I have left here!

Brace of pheasants . . . an anchovy!

BARDOLPH

(*taking coins out of the purse and putting them on the table*)

A shilling, a shilling, a penny.

FALSTAFF

Go on!

BARDOLPH

This is all, Sir.

FALSTAFF

Nonsense!

BARDOLPH

(*throwing the purse on the table*)

See . . . there is not a penny left!

FALSTAFF (*rising*)

Ah, you lout, you destroy me!

Week after week I spend ten guineas to indulge you, you drunkard!

Night after night I ponder,
As from inn to inn we wander,
How your monstrous nose can yield the glow
To guide me here and yonder.
But what I save on lamp-oil
You waste on drink and dining.
So for thirty long years I keep
Your fiery nose a-shining!

You're too costly.

(*to Pistol, then to the innkeeper*)

And you also. Ho there! A flagon of sherry!

(*to Bardolph and Pistol*)

You are threatening my substance.
A weak and slender Falstaff
Is not himself! A fearsome nightmare!
For in this paunch here you will find all the reasons for my immortal glory.

PISTOL (*assenting*)

Falstaff the Mighty!

BARDOLPH

Tremendous Falstaff!

FALSTAFF

(*looking at himself and patting his paunch*)

This royal treasure, I'll make it grow!

The mind, though, no longer yield to matter!

BARDOLPH, PISTOL

Then let us think!

(*all three in a huddle*)

FALSTAFF

There lives in town a certain gentleman whose name is Ford.

BARDOLPH

Yes.

PISTOL

Yes.

FALSTAFF

A man of wealth and of distinction.

PISTOL

Most wealthy and most gen'rous.

BARDOLPH

A lord!

FALSTAFF

His wife has beauty . . .

PISTOL

. . . and holds the purse-strings . . .

FALSTAFF

. . . such beauty! Oh, love!

Starlike her eyes! Swanlike her bosom!

Like blossoms her rosy lips beguiling!

Her name is Alice. One morning she saw me from her window, and I beheld her smiling!

Then lightning struck in the deep of my heart.

Divine, her radiant eyes turned their brilliant and blinding light on me, on me!

(*strutting*)

On chest and shoulders, on legs like boulders,

This paunch so proud, this manly stature, noble, imposing.

And then her glance, aglow with wild desire, would plainly tell me what I hoped to hear:

"I love you, Sir John Falstaff!"

BARDOLPH

Unquote!

FALSTAFF

Yet, hear me: There's someone . . .

BARDOLFO, PISTOLA

Un'altra?

FALSTAFF

E questa ha nome: Margherita.

PISTOLA

La chiaman Meg.

FALSTAFF

È anch'essa de' miei pregi invaghita.
E anch'essa tien le chiavi dello scrigno.
Costoro
Saran le mie Golconde e le mie Coste
d'oro!
Guardate. Io sono ancora una piacente
estate
Di San Martino. A voi, due lettere in-
fuocate.

(*Dà a Bardolfo una delle due lettere
che sono rimaste sul tavolo*).

Tu porta questa a Meg; tentiam la sua
virtù.

(*Bardolfo prende la lettera.*)

Già vedo che il tuo naso arde di zelo.

(*a Pistola, porgendogli l'altra lettera*)

E tu porta questa ad Alice.

PISTOLA

(*ricusando con dignità*)

Porto una spada al fianco.
Non sono un Messer Pandarus. Ricuso.

FALSTAFF

(*con calma sprezzante*)

Saltimbanco.

BARDOLFO

(*avanzandosi e gettando la lettera sul
tavolo*)

Sir John, in quest'intrigo non posso ac-
condiscendervi.
Lo vieta . . .

FALSTAFF (*interrompendolo*)

Chi?

BARDOLFO

L'Onore.

FALSTAFF

(*vedendo il paggio Robin che entra dal
fondo*)

Ehi! paggio!

(*poi subito a Bardolfo e Pistola*)

Andate a impendervi, ma non più a me!

(*al paggio che escirà correndo colle
lettere*)

Due lettere, prendi, per due signore.
Consegna tosto, corri,
Via, lesto, va!

(*rivolto a Pistola e Bardolfo*)

L'Onore! Ladri!
Voi state ligi all'onor vostro, voi!
Cloache d'ignominia, quando, non
sempre, noi
Possiam star ligi al nostro. Io stesso, sì,
io, io,
Devo talor da un lato porre il timor di
Dio
E, per necessità, sviar l'onore, usare
Stratagemmi ed equivoci, destreggiar,
bordeggiare.
E voi, coi vostri cenci e coll'occhiata
tôrta
Da gatto-pardo e i fetidi sghignazzi
avete a scorta
Il vostro Onor! Che onore?! che onor?
che onor! che ciancia!
Che baia! Può l'onore riempirvi la
pancia?
No. Può l'onor rimettervi uno stinco?
Non puo.
Nè un piede? No. Nè un dito? No. Nè
un capello? No.
L'onor non è chirurgo. Che è dunque?
Una parola.
Che c'è in questa parola? C'è dell'aria
che vola.
Bel costrutto! L'onore lo può sentir chi
è morto?
No. Vive sol coi vivi? . . . Neppure:
perchè a torto
Lo gonfian le lusinghe, lo corrompe
l'orgoglio,
L'ammorban le calunnie; e per me non
ne voglio!
Ma, per tornare a voi, furfanti,
ho atteso troppo,
E vi discaccio.

(*Prende in mano la scopa e insegue
Bardolfo e Pistola che scansano i
colpi correndo qua e là e riparandosi
dietro la tavola.*)

Olà! Lesti! Lesti! al galoppo!
Al galoppo! Il capestro assai bene vi sta.

BARDOLPH, PISTOL

Another?

FALSTAFF

. . . her name, it seems, is Mistress Page.

PISTOL

They call her Meg.

FALSTAFF

For her, too, I hold a fatal fascination,
and darling Meg is mistress . . .

ALL THREE

. . . of the purse-strings!

FALSTAFF

These beauties on wings of gold
shall take Sir John to Eldorado.
Behold me! I shall yet be the knight in
shining armor who will redeem you!
And you shall expedite the matter:
(*handing Bardolph one of the two letters on the table*)
This letter take to Meg. Her virtue shall
be tried!
(*Bardolph takes the letter.*)
I see: Your fiery nose glows at the
prospect.
(*to Pistol, tending him the other letter*)
And you, you bring this one to Alice!

PISTOL

(*refusing with dignity*)

No! By my sword, I shall not!
A low and shameful go-between? No,
never!

FALSTAFF

(*with calm contempt*)

Ah, you windbag!

BARDOLPH

(*stepping forth and depositing the letter
on the table*)

Sir John, in this endeavor you must
proceed without me.
I'm bound by . . .

FALSTAFF (*interrupting him*)

. . . what?

BARDOLPH

. . . my honor.

FALSTAFF

(*noticing the page, Robin, just entering
the door*)

Hey, Robin!
(*turns to Bardolph and Pistol*)
Get out and hang yourselves . . . but not
on me!

(*to the page who takes the letters and
runs off*)

These letters here, take them to two
young ladies.
Go, take them quickly, hurry, go!
Fly, scurry, go!
(*turning back to Bardolph and Pistol*)
Your honor? Scoundrels!

FALSTAFF

You dare to speak to me of honor?
You?
You foul and filthy mongrels . . .
When on occasion *we* may find our own
in peril?
I . . . listen: *I* have had to hide my
glances, asking the grace of Heaven,
as in the throes of need I pawned my
honor, sought refuge in some guile or
some deception, in a ruse or a false-
hood.
And you, decrepit wretches, you stink-
ing, vile hyenas who feed on carrion,
you putrified rapscallions,
You speak of honor . . . and this to me?
What honor? Speak up! Come on, you
idiots, you asses!
Can your honor fill your paunch when
it's empty? No!
Or can honor cure a broken ankle? Oh
no!
A finger? No. A toenail? No! Or a
whisker? No.
For honor is no surgeon.
What is it? Only a word!
What is it, what is it really?
Just a breeze that will vanish. . . .
Fancy fiction!
A dead man, can he take pride in
honor? No!
Yet he who is living? Not either.
For he who owns it has no way to de-
fend it.
It is frail and will crumble, killed off by
human weakness.
Therefore I do not want it, no, do not
want it, no! No, no!
But to return to you, you scoundrels:
I've been too lenient. I now dismiss you.

(*He grabs the broom and chases Bardolph and Pistol around the room.
They try to hide behind the table.*)

Away! Quickly, scurry! I shall teach
you how to hurry.
From the gallows you'll soon swing and
sway.

Ladri! Via! Via di qua!
Via di qua! Via di qua!

(*Bardolfo fugge dalla porta a sinistra.
Pistola fugge dall'uscio del fondo, non
senza essersi buscato qualche colpo di
granata, e Falstaff lo insegue.*)

PARTE SECONDA

(*Giardino. A sinistra la casa di Ford.
Gruppi d'alberi nel centro della
scena.*

*Alice, Nannetta, Meg, Mrs. Quickly,
poi Mr. Ford, Fenton, Dr. Cajus,
Bardolfo, Pistola.*

*Meg con Mrs. Quickly da destra.
S'avviano verso la casa di Ford, e
sulla soglia s'imbattono in Alice e
Nannetta che stanno per escire.*)

MEG
Alice.

ALICE
Meg.

MEG
Nannetta.

ALICE
Escivo appunto per ridere con te.

(*a Mrs. Quickly*)

Buon dì, comare.

QUICKLY
Dio vi doni allegria.

(*accarezzando la guancia di Nannetta*)

Botton di rosa!

ALICE (*ancora a Meg*)
Giungi in buon punto.
M'accade un fatto da trasecolare.

MEG
Anche a me.

QUICKLY
(*che parlava con Nannetta, avvicinandosi con curiosità*)

Che?

NANNETTA (*avvicinandosi*)
Che cosa?

ALICE (*a Meg*)
Narra il tuo caso.

MEG
Narra il tuo.

ALICE (*in crocchio*)
Promessa di non ciarlar.

MEG
Ti pare?!

QUICKLY
Oibò! Vi pare?!

ALICE
Dunque: se m'acconciassi a entrar ne'
    rei
Propositi del diavolo, sarei
Promossa al grado di Cavalleressa!

MEG
Anch'io.

ALICE
Motteggi.

MEG
(*Cerca in tasca: estrae una lettera.*)
Non più parole,
Chè qui sciupiamo la luce del sole.
Ho una lettera.

ALICE
Anch'io.

NANNETTA, QUICKLY
Oh!!

ALICE
Leggi. (*Dà la lettera a Meg.*)

MEG
(*Scambia la propria lettera con quella
    d' Alice.*)
Leggi.
    (*leggendo la lettera d' Alice*)
«Fulgida Alice! amor t'offro . . .»
. . . Ma come?! Che cosa dice?
Salvo che il nome la frase è uguale.

ALICE
(*Cogli occhi sulla lettera che tiene in
    mano, ripete la lettura di Meg.*)
«Fulgida Meg! amor t'offro . . .»

MEG
(*continuando sul proprio foglio la let-
    tura d'Alice.*)
«. . . amor bramo»

ALICE
Qua Meg, là Alice.

MEG
È tal e quale.
«Non domandar perchè ma dimmi:

Robbers, scoundrels, rascals, bandits!
If you stay you will pay. Go away! On
your way!

(*Bardolph flees through the door at the
left, Pistol through the center after
having received some blows. Falstaff
follows Pistol out the door.*)

Part Two

*A Garden. To the left Ford's house. A
group of trees center-stage. Alice,
Ann, Meg, Mrs. Quickly, later Ford,
Fenton, Dr. Cajus, Bardolph, and
Pistol.*

(*Meg and Mrs. Quickly enter from the
right and cross towards Ford's house
on whose threshold they encounter
Alice and Ann just leaving the
house.*)

MEG

Oh, Alice!

ALICE

Meg!

MEG

Good morning!

ALICE

I'm glad you're here for I was on my
way to you.

(*to Mrs. Quickly*)

Good day, Dame Quickly!

QUICKLY

Heaven grant you good fortune!

(*patting Ann's cheek*)

My Ann, my rosebud!

ALICE

(*still speaking to Meg*)

Now let me tell you:
I am amazed at something that occurred.

MEG

So am I.

QUICKLY

(*having conversed with Ann, now approaching inquisitively*)

What?

ANN

(*coming closer, too*)

What was it?

ALICE (*to Meg*)

Speak out and tell me!

MEG

No, I listen.

ALICE (*mysteriously*)

But promise: No word of this!

MEG

Of course not!

QUICKLY

Oh no! Of course not!

ALICE

Hear then: If I were willing to make a
naughty bargain
With the Devil, my sin would be re-
warded with the rank of Lady!

MEG

Mine also!

ALICE

You're joking!

MEG

(*drawing a letter out of her pocket*)

Why go on talking when we should call
on the sunlight to help us? I have a
letter.

ALICE

I also.

ANN, QUICKLY

Oh?

ALICE

Read it!

(*gives her letter to Meg.*)

MEG

(*exchanging her own letter with that of
Alice*)

Read it!

(*reading Alice's letter*)

"Exquisite Alice! I adore you. . . ."
What is this? I can't believe it.
But for the name the words are the
same.

ALICE

(*her eyes on the letter in her hand, re-
peats the contents of Meg's letter*)

"Exquisite Meg! I adore you. . . ."

MEG

(*reading the letter in her hand*)

"I implore you . . ."

ALICE

Here "Meg", there "Alice"!

MEG

Letter for letter!
"Ah, do not ask why, but say. . . ."

ALICE

. . . t'amo.»
Pur non gli offersi cagion.

MEG

Il nostro caso è pur strano.
(*Tutte in un gruppo addosso alle lettere, confrontandole e maneggian-
dole con curiosità.*)

QUICKLY

Guardiam con flemma.

MEG

Gli stessi versi.

ALICE

Lo stesso inchiostro.

QUICKLY

La stessa mano.

NANNETTA

Lo stesso stemma.

ALICE, MEG

(*leggendo insieme ciascuna sulla pro-
pria lettera*)
«Sei la gaia comare, il compar gaio
«Son io, e fra noi due facciamo il paio».

ALICE

Già.

NANNETTA

Lui, lei, te.

QUICKLY

Un paio in tre.

ALICE

«Facciamo il paio in un amor ridente»
«Di donna bella e d'uom appariscente»

TUTTE

Appariscente . . .»

ALICE

"E il viso tuo su me risplenderà come
una stella sul immensità.

TUTTE (*ridendo*)

Ah! Ah! Ah! Ah! Ah! Ah! Ah! Ah!

ALICE

«Rispondi al tuo scudiere,
John Falstaff Cavaliere».

QUICKLY

Mostro!

ALICE

Dobbiam gabbarlo.

NANNETTA

E farne chiasso.

ALICE

E metterlo in burletta.

NANNETTA

Oh! Oh! che spasso!

QUICKLY

Che allegria!

MEG

Che vendetta!

(*rivolgendosi or all'una ora all'altra, tutte in crocchio cinguettando*)

ALICE

Quell'otre! quel tino!
Quel Re delle pancie,
Ci ha ancora le ciance
Del bel vagheggino.
E l'olio gli sgocciola
Dall'adipe unticcio
E ancor ei ne snocciola
La strofa e il bisticcio!
Lasciam ch'ei le pronte
Sue ciarle ne spifferi;
Farà come i pifferi
Che sceser dal monte.
Vedrai che, se abbindolo
Quel grosso compar,
Più lesto d'un guindolo
Lo faccio girar.

QUICKLY (*ad Alice*)

Quell'uom è un cannone!
Se scoppia, ci spaccia.
Colui, se l'abbraccia,
Ti schiaccia Giunone.
Ma certo si spappola
Quel mostro a tuo cenno
E corre alla trappola
E perde il suo senno.
Potenza d'un fragile
Sorriso di donna!
Scïenza d'un'agile
Movenza di gonna!
Se il vischio lo impegola
Lo udremo strillar,
E allor la sua fregola
Vedremo svampar.

ALICE
". . . I love you!"
I cannot see what this means.

MEG
I find it all most confusing.
(*All in the group crowd around the
letters, perusing them and fingering
them with great interest.*)

QUICKLY
Let's not be hasty!

MEG
The same expressions!

ALICE
Alike the writing!

QUICKLY
Even the paper.

ANN
Everything matches.

ALICE, MEG
(*reading jointly, each her own letter*)
"You are cheerful and charming,
I debonair and disarming:
We are a pair joined by our fortune."

ALICE
Well!

ANN
She . . . you . . . he . . .

QUICKLY
. . . a pair of three!

ALICE
" . . . in love united
a pair of doves so tender,
the fairest lady . . . "

ALL
". . . a man of weight and splendor!"

ALICE
"Your radiant beauty on me will shed
    its light
As bright and smiling out of the sky
A star will shine at night."

ALL (*laughing*)
Ha, ha, ha, ha.

ALICE
"Reply to your admirer!
Your servant, Sir John Falstaff."

ALL
Monster!

ALICE
We must defy him . . .

ANN
. . . and twit and taunt him . . .

ALICE
. . . We'll fool him and we'll chide him.

ANN
. . . and hit and haunt him!

QUICKLY
We will cool him . . .

MEG
. . . and deride him!

(*turning from one to the other, all huddling together*)

ALICE
This monstrous decanter,
This prince of dilation,
Shall harvest vexation
From frolic and banter!
His crass notoriety
Will be his perdition,
We'll teach him sobriety
But cause no suspicion.
He'll follow us gladly
And tumble more readily
For he who courts headily
Will often court badly.
Watch out, you polygamist
Disguished as a vat:
The fate of a bigamist,
A tri- or tetragamist,
Is something to fear,
Above all when you're fat!

QUICKLY
(*to Alice*)
That gun with its thunder,
We'll dampen its powder
And laugh even louder
While calling its blunder!
But as you pursue him
And shrewdly ensnare him
Before you undo him
You better beware him:
He's artful and wily,
Of canny felinity,
And may trick your trinity
Unless you act slyly!
For all his fatuity
He's quick as a cat.
'T will take ingenuity
And great assiduity
To puncture his pride
And to batter him flat.

NANNETTA (*ad Alice*)

Se ordisci una burla,
Vo' anch'io la mia parte.
Conviene condurla
Con senno, con arte.
L'agguato ov'ei sdrucciola
Convien ch'ei non scerna;
Già prese una lucciola
Per una lanterna.
Che il gioco riesca
Pericò più non dubito;
Poi coglierlo subito.
Bisogna offrir l'esca
E se i scilinguagnoli
Sapremo adoprar,
Vedremo a rigagnoli
Quell'orco sudar.

MEG

Un flutto in tempesta
Gittò sulla rena
Di Windsor codesta
Vorace balena.
Ma qui non ha spazio
Da farsi più pingue;
Ne fecer già strazio
Le vostre tre lingue.
Tre lingue più allegre
D'un trillo di nacchere,
Che spargon più chiacchiere
Di sei cingallegre.
Tal sempre s'esilari
Quel bel cinguettar.
Così soglion l'ilari
Comari ciarlar.

(*S'allontanano.*)

(*Mr. Ford, Dr. Cajus, Fenton, Bardolfo, Pistola entrano da destra, mentre le donne escono da sinistra. Ford nel centro, Pistola al suo fianco destro, Bardolfo al suo fianco sinistro, Fenton e il Dr. Cajus dietro Ford. Tutti in gruppo, parlando a Ford a basso voce, e brontolando.*)

DR. CAJUS

È un ribaldo, un furbo, un ladro,
Un furfante, un turco, un vandalo;
L'altro dì mandò a soqquadro
La mia casa e fu uno scandalo.
Se un processo oggi gl'intavolo
Sconterà le sue rapine,
Ma la sua più degna fine
Sia d'andare in man del diavolo.
E quei due che avete accanto
Genti son di sua tribù,
Non son due stinchi di santo
Nè son fiori di virtù.

BARDOLFO

Falstaff, sì, ripeto, giuro,
(Per mia bocca il ciel v'illumina)
Contro voi John Falstaff rumina
Un progetto alquanto impuro.
Son uom d'arme e quèll'infame
Più non vo' che v'impozzangheri;
Non vorrei, no, escir dai gangheri
Dell'onor per un reame!
Messer Ford, l'uomo avvisato
Non è salvo che a metà.
Tocca a voi d'ordir l'agguato
Che l'agguato stornerà.

FORD

(*da sè, poi agli altri*)

Un ronzio di vespe e d'avidi
Calabron brontolamento,
Un rombar di nembi gravidi
D'uragani è quel ch'io sento.
Il cerèbro un ebro allucina
Turbamento di paura;
Ciò che intorno a me si buccina,
È un susurro di congiura.
Parlan quattro ed uno ascolta;
Qual dei quattro ascolterò?
Se parlaste uno alla volta
Forse allor v'intenderò.

ANN (*to Alice*)

Oh, let me, dear Mother,
Share frolic and laughter.
This game like no other
Will ring down the rafter.
Denying our amity
We'll gaily forsake him,
And blackest calamity
Will soon overtake him.
His silly pretensions,
His shaky morality
Increase his mortality
To dreadful dimensions.
You symbol of vanity,
You lecher, you gnat,
We'll bring you to sanity,
Respect and urbanity,
Yes, all these you'll learn
As we hand you your hat!

MEG

Come up from the ocean
To harry and hound us
A monster has bound us
In fear and commotion.
So let's be unanimous
And plan our defences!
This man pusillanimous
Let's bring to his senses!
Our ways must be cunning,
Discreet and believable.
Our end is achievable,
Hilarious and stunning.
Your shameless duplicity,
You scoundrel, you rat,
Will bring us felicity
And bring you publicity . . .
You'll never again
Want to bargain for that!

(*They all exit.*)

(*Mr. Ford, Dr. Cajus, Fenton, Bardolph, and Pistol enter from the right while the women exit on the left. Ford is in the center, on his right Pistol, and Bardolph on his left. Fenton and Cajus are behind Ford. They all converge on Ford, whispering to him in great agitation.*)

DR. CAJUS

He's a liar and a lecher,
All he knows is rape and robbery.
He's a lout and rake and retcher
And a paragon of snobbery.
He has broken all my crockery,
Whipped my mare until she's dying.
Devil take him. keep him frying
As reward for all his mockery.
These two rascals here beside you:
They are evil through and through.
Let my friendly council guide you:
I'd beware if I were you!

BARDOLPH

Falstaff, as I keep repeating,
Is a genius at cheating.
Master Ford, let me reiterate:
It is you he will obliterate.
I'm a soldier but no booty
Ever dulls my sensitivity
And compels me to activity
Which offends my sense of duty.
Master Ford, I know you need me:
Let my warning come in time:
It is you who now must heed me
To prevent this ugly crime!

FORD

(*to himself, then to the others*)

Ah, around me all this flummery
Has begun to overcome me
Like a bumbling kind of mummery
Which will stun me and benumb me.
How I wish they would be sensible
So I'd know what each is doing!
Though they are incomprehensible
I can feel a danger brewing.
I should highly praise and cheer you
If you only were aware:
Four to speak and one to hear you . . .
This indeed is hardly fair!

PISTOLA

Sir John Falstaff già v'appresta,
Messer Ford, un gran pericolo.
Già vi pende sulla testa
Qualche cosa a perpendicolo.
Messer Ford, fui già un armigero
Di quell'uom dall'ampia cute;
Or mi pento e mi morigero
Per ragioni di salute.
La minaccia or v'è scoperta,
Or v'è noto il ciurmador.
State all'erta, all'erta, all'erta!
Qui si tratta dell'onor.

FENTON

Se volete, io non mi perito
Di ridurlo alla ragione
Colle brusche o colle buone,
E pagarlo al par del merito.
Mi dà il cuore e mi solletica
(E sarà una giostra gaia)
Di sfondar quella ventraia
Iperbolico-apoplettica.
Col consiglio o colla spada
Se lo trovo al tu per tu,
O lui va per la sua strada
O lo assegno a Belzebù.

FORD (*a Pistola*)

Ripeti.

PISTOLA (*a Ford*)

In due parole:
L'enorme Falstaff vuole
Entrar nel vostro tetto,
Beccarvi la consorte,
Sfondar la cassa-forte
E sconquassarvi il letto.

DR. CAJUS

Caspita!

FORD

Quanti guai!

BARDOLFO (*a Ford*)

Già le scrisse un biglietto . . .

PISTOLA

Ma quel messaggio abbietto
Ricusai.

BARDOLFO

Ricusai.

PISTOLA

Badate a voi!

BARDOLFO

Badate!

PISTOLA

Falstaff le occhieggia tutte
Che siano belle o brutte,
Pulzelle o maritate.

BARDOLFO

La corona che adorna
D'Atteòn l'irte chiome
Su voi già spunta.

FORD

Come sarebbe a dir?

BARDOLFO

Le corna.

FORD

Brutta parola!

DR. CAJUS

Ha voglie voraci il Cavaliere.

FORD

Sorveglierò la moglie.
Sorveglierò il messere.
(*Rientrano da sinistra le quattro
donne.*)
Salvar vo' i beni miei
Dagli appetiti altrui.

FENTON (*vedendo Nannetta*)

È lei.

NANNETTA (*vedendo Fenton*)

È lui.

FORD (*vedendo Alice*)

È lei.

ALICE (*vedendo Ford*)

È lui.

DR. CAJUS
(*a Ford, indicando Alice*)

È lei.

MEG
(*ad Alice, indicando Ford*)

È lui.

ALICE
(*alle altre, a bassa voce, indicando
Ford*)

S'egli sapesse!

NANNETTA

Guai!

ALICE

Schiviamo i passi suoi.

MEG

Ford è geloso?

ALICE

Assai.

PISTOL

Every man in town will scorn you.
Falstaff has a plan perfidious
For he wishes to adorn you
With a headgear worse than hideous.
I know well I was unsavory.
Falstaff made me lose my senses.
I repent and hope my bravery
Will atone for my offences.
There is nothing more to mention,
Now the rest is up to you:
Be on guard and pay attention
And find out what he will do!

FENTON

For his scandalous temerity
I should like to see him suffer.
And my fury and severity
Will defeat the brazen bluffer.
And my heart flies high and higher,
I can feel my senses quivering
When I think of that old liar
On his knees, all spent and shivering.
I will first appeal to reason
But if this should not do well,
Then it would amount to treason
Not to send him down to Hell!

FORD (to Pistol)

Continue!

PISTOL (to Ford)

I'll tell you shortly:
Sir Falstaff round and portly
Is yearning for some headroom.
Your till could be his treasure,
Your wife provide his pleasure
While he commands your bedroom!

DR. CAJUS

Dash it all!

FORD

Ah, I'll die!

BARDOLPH (to Ford)

And a letter he penned her. . . .

PISTOL

. . . through me he meant to send her.
'No!' said I.

BARDOLPH

So did I.

PISTOL

So be on guard!

BARDOLPH

Remember: . . .

PISTOL

For him no woman's holy,
Tall, lean, or roly-poly,
In May or in December!

BARDOLPH

Or the crowning adornment of Actae-
on's fair brow
Will be found on you, Sir.

FORD

What do you mean by that?

BARDOLPH

The horns, Sir!

FORD

Ghastly expression!

DR. CAJUS

The gentleman's greed shocks me
indeed!

FORD

My wife and that old charmer,
That knight in rusting armor:
(The four women re-enter from the
left.)
She still belongs to me,
This much I guarantee!

FENTON (noticing Ann)

'Tis she!

ANN (noticing Fenton)

'Tis he!

FORD (noticing Alice)

'Tis she!

ALICE (noticing Ford)

'Tis he!

DR. CAJUS
(to Ford, pointing to Alice)

'Tis she!

MEG
(to Alice, pointing to Ford)

'Tis he!

ALICE
(to the others, referring to Ford)

If he should guess it . . .!

ANN

My! . . .

ALICE

We'd better now avoid him.

MEG

Why? Is he jealous?

ALICE

Insanely.

QUICKLY

Zitto.

ALICE

Badiamo a noi?.

(*Alice, Meg e Quickly escono da sinistra. Resta Nannetta. Ford, Dr. Cajus, Bardolfo e Pistola escono da destra. Resta Fenton.*)

FENTON

(*fra i cespugli, verso Nannetta, a bassa voce*)

Pst, pst, Nannetta.

NANNETTA

(*mettendo l'indice al labbro per cenno di silenzio*)

Ssss.

FENTON

Vien qua.

NANNETTA

(*guardando attorno con cautela*)

Taci. Che vuoi?

FENTON

Due baci.

NANNETTA

In fretta.

FENTON

In fretta.

(*Si baciano rapidamente.*)

NANNETTA

Labbra di foco!

FENTON

Labbra di fiore! . . .

NANNETTA

Che il vago gioco sanno d'amore.

FENTON

Che spargon ciarle, che mostran perle,
Belle a vederle, dolci a baciarle!

(*Tenta di abbracciarla.*)

Labbra leggiadre!

NANNETTA

(*difendendosi e guardandosi attorno*)

Man malandrine!

FENTON

Ciglia assassine!
Pupille ladre!
T'amo! (*Fa per baciarla ancora.*)

NANNETTA

Imprudente. No.

FENTON

Sì . . . Due baci.

NANNETTA (*Si svincola.*)

Basta.

FENTON

Mi piaci tanto!

NANNETTA

Vien gente.

(*Si allontanano l'una dall'altro, mentre ritornano le donne.*)

FENTON

(*cantando allontanandosi*)

«Bocca baciata non perde ventura.»

NANNETTA

(*continuando il canto di Fenton, avvicinandosi alle altre donne*)

«Anzi rinnova come fa la luna.»

ALICE

Falstaff m'ha canzonata.

MEG

Merita un gran castigo.

ALICE

Se gli scrivessi un rigo? . . .

NANNETTA

(*riunendosi al crocchio con disinvoltura*)

Val meglio un'ambasciata.

ALICE

Sì.

QUICKLY

Sì.

ALICE (*a Quickly*)

Da quel brigante tu andrai.
Lo adeschi all'offa d'un ritrovo galante
con me.

QUICKLY

Questa è gaglioffa!

NANNETTA

Che bella burla!

ALICE

Prima per attirarlo a noi lo
lusinghiamo.

NANNETTA

E poi?

ALICE

E poi gliele cantiamo in rima.

QUICKLY

Non merita riguardo.

ALICE

È un bove.

QUICKLY

Silence!

ALICE

We'd better hide!

(Alice, Meg, and Quickly exit to the left. Ford, Dr. Cajus, Bardolph and Pistol exit to the right. Ann and Fenton remain on stage.)

FENTON

(from the bushes, softly calling Ann)

Pst! Ann! My darling, come here!

ANN

(putting her forefinger to her lips to caution him)

Quiet! 'Tis you?

FENTON

Come, kiss me!

ANN

But quickly!

FENTON

Yes, quickly!

(rapid exchange of kisses)

ANN

Lips, oh so burning!

FENTON

Lips red as roses!

ANN

Lips where my yearning
sweetly reposes!

FENTON

Sometimes revealing
pearls shining brightly,
Kissing me lightly,
wounding or healing!
Kisses that haunt me . . . (tries to embrace her)

ANN

(defending herself and looking around)

Brazen offender!

FENTON

Glances so tender,
Why do you taunt me?
Kiss me. . . . (tries to kiss her again)

ANN

They will hear us! No . . .

FENTON

Please . . . two kisses!

ANN (freeing herself)

Rascal!

FENTON

Ah, how I love you!

ANN

They're near us.

(They leave each other while the women re-enter.)

FENTON

(hiding behind the bushes)

"Just kiss me soon,
and you always will do it!"

ANN

(continuing Fenton's song while approaching the women)

"Trust in the moon,
love will always renew it!"

ALICE

Falstaff tells us a fable.

MEG

Wait till we turn the table!

ALICE

What if I wrote a letter?

(rejoining the women in an off-hand manner)

ANN

A messenger were better.

ALICE

Yes.

QUICKLY

Yes.

ALICE (to Quickly)

The one to see him is you,
And you invite him to a tender appointment with me.

QUICKLY

This will excite him.

ANN

It will delight him.

ALICE

First we will bait a trap to lure him and secure him.

ANN

And then?

ALICE

And then . . . and then we'll let him have it!

QUICKLY

A long belated matter!

That bulldog!

ALICE

MEG

È un uomo senza fede.

ALICE

È un monte di lardo.

MEG

Non merita clemenza.

ALICE

È un ghiotton che scialacqua
Tutto il suo aver nel cuoco.

NANNETTA

Lo tufferem nell'acqua.

ALICE

Lo arrostiremo al fuoco.

NANNETTA

Che gioia!

ALICE

Che allegria!

MEG (*a Quickly*)

Procaccia di far bene la tua parte.

QUICKLY

(*accorgendosi di Fenton che s'aggira
nel fondo*)
Chi viene?

MEG

Là c'è qualcun che spia.
(*Escono rapidamente da destra Alice,
Meg, Quickly. Nannetta resta,
Fenton le torna accanto.*)

FENTON

Torno all'assalto.

NANNETTA (*come sfidandolo*)

Torno alla gara. Ferisci!

FENTON

Para!
(*Si slancia per baciarla: Nannetta si
ripara il viso con una mano che Fenton bacia e vorrebbe ribaciare; ma
Nannetta la solleva più alta che può
e Fenton ritenta invano di raggiun-
gerla colle labbra.*)

NANNETTA

La mira è in alto.
L'amor è un agile
Torneo, sua corte
Vuol che il più fragile
Vinca il più forte.

FENTON

M'armo, ti guardo.
T'aspetto al varco.

NANNETTA

Il labbro è l'arco.

FENTON

E il bacio è il dardo.
Bada! la freccia
Fatal già scocca
Dalla mia bocca
Sulla tua treccia. (*Le bacia la treccia.*)

NANNETTA

(*annodandogli il collo colla treccia,
mentre egli la bacia*)
Eccoti avvinto.

FENTON

Chiedo la vita!

NANNETTA

Io son ferita,
Ma tu sei vinto.

FENTON

Pietà! Facciamo la pace e poi.

NANNETTA

E poi?

FENTON

Se vuoi, ricominciamo.

NANNETTA

Bello è quel gioco
Che dura poco. Basta.

FENTON

Amor mio!

NANNETTA

Vien gente. Addio!
(*Fugge da destra.*)

FENTON

(*allontanandosi cantando*)
«Bocca baciata non perde ventura.»

NANNETTA

(*di dentro rispondendo*)
«Anzi rinnova come fa la luna.»
(*Rientrano dal fondo Ford, Dr. Cajus,
Bardolfo, Pistola. Fenton si unisce
poi al crocchio.*)

BARDOLFO (*a Ford*)

Udrai quanta egli sfoggia magnilo-
quenza altera.

FORD

Diceste ch'egli alloggia . . . Dove?

PISTOLA

Alla Giarrettiera.

MEG
That miscreant seducer!

ALICE
That mountain of batter!

MEG
We'll show him no compassion.

ALICE
He keeps eating and drinking
until his senses fail him.

ANN
We'll dunk him till he's sinking . . .

ALICE
. . . and boil and roast and scale him!

ANN
Delightful!

ALICE
This is priceless!

MEG (*to Quickly*)
You know your part,
now play it to perfection!

QUICKLY
(*noticing Fenton hiding nearby*)
Who is this?

MEG
Beware! There's someone spying!
(*The women, except Ann, rapidly exit
to the right. Fenton comes forward as
soon as they are gone.*)

FENTON
Now I shall storm you.

ANN
(*pretending to defy him*)
You won't embrace me. Just try it!

FENTON
Face me!
(*He tries to kiss her. She covers her face
with her hand which Fenton kisses.
Then she raises her hand too high for
him to reach it with his lips.*)

ANN
I shall reform you.
In love the frail and fair defender
Will in the end be victorious
And will win surrender.

FENTON
Soon I shall bind you
And shall disarm you.

ANN
But I will charm you.

FENTON
My kiss will find you.
Careful! Your tresses
So soft and tender
Will now surrender
To my caresses. (*He kisses her hair.*)

ANN
(*puts one of her tresses around his neck,
as if to capture him*)
Caught is the sinner!

FENTON
Ah, heed my pleading!

ANN
Wounded and bleeding,
I am the winner.

FENTON
I yield the field, hand over my weapon,
and then . . .

ANN
. . . and then?

FENTON
And then we start it all over.

ANN
Let me invite you!
I love to fight you . . . later!

FENTON
Do not flee me!

ANN
I hear them . . . they'll see me!
(*off to the right*)

FENTON
(*while withdrawing*)
"Just kiss me soon,
and you always will do it!"

ANN
(*answering him from offstage*)
"Trust in the moon,
love will always renew it!"
(*Re-enter Ford, Dr. Cajus, Bardolph,
and Pistol. Fenton rejoins them pres-
ently.*)

BARDOLPH (*to Ford*)
To listen to his braying
makes any man a martyr.

FORD
You mentioned where he's staying . . .
tell me!

PISTOL
Close by, at the "Garter".

FORD

O lui mi annuncierete,
Ma con un falso nome;
Poscia vedrete come
Lo piglio nella rete.
Ma... non una parola.

BARDOLFO

In ciarle non m'ingolfo.
Io mi chiamo Bardolfo.

PISTOLA

Io mi chiamo Pistola.

FORD

Siam d'accordo.

BARDOLFO

L'arcano custodirem.

PISTOLA

Son sordo e muto.

FORD

Siam d'accordo tutti.

BARDOLFO, PISTOLA

Sì.

(*Si avanzano nel fondo Alice, Nannetta, Meg, Quickly.*)

DR. CAJUS (*a Ford*)

Del tuo barbaro diagnostico
Forse il male è assai men barbaro.
Ti convien tentar la prova
Molestissima del ver.
Così avvien col sapor ostico
Del ginepro e del rabarbaro;
Il benessere rinnova
L'amarissimo bicchier.

PISTOLA (*a Ford*)

Voi dovete empirgli il calice,
Tratto, tratto interrogandolo,
Per tentar se vi riesca
Di trovar del nodo il bandolo.
Come all'acqua inclina il salice,
Così al vin quel Cavalier.
Scoverete la sua tresca,
Scoprirete il suo pensier.

FORD (*a Pistola*)

Tu vedrai se bene adopera
L'arte mia con quell'infame.
E sarà prezzo dell'opera
S'io discopro le sue trame.
Se da me storno il ridicolo
Non avrem sudato invan.
S'io mi salvo dal pericolo,
L'angue morde il cerretan.

BARDOLFO (*a Ford*)

Messer Ford, un infortunio
Marital in voi s'incorpora;
Se non siete astuto e cauto
Quel Sir John vi tradirà
Quel paffuto plenilunio
Che il color del vino imporpora
Troverebbe un pasto lauto
Nella vostra ingenuità.

FENTON (*fra sè*)

Qua borbotta un crocchio d'uomini,
C'è nell'aria una malìa.
Là cinguetta un stuol di femine,
Spira un vento agitator.
Ma colei che in cor mi nomini,
Dolce amor, vuol esser mia!
Noi sarem come due gemine
Stelle unite in un ardor.

ALICE (*a Meg*)

Vedrai che, se abbindolo
Quel grosso compar.
Più lesto d'un guindolo
Lo faccio girar.

MEG (*ad Alice*)

Se il vischio lo impegola
Lo undremo strillar,
E allor la sua fregola
Vedremo svampar.

NANNETTA (*ad Alice*)

E se i scilinguagnoli
Sapremo adoprar,
Vedremo a rigagnoli
Quell'orco sudar.

QUICKLY

Tal sempre s'esilari
Quel bel cinguettar;
Così soglion l'ilari
Comari ciarlar.

(*Ford, Dr. Cajus, Fenton, Bardolfo, Pistola escono.*)

FORD

You ask him to receive me,
Hiding my name and station!
John Falstaff's castigation
Is under way, believe me!
If you're discreet and loyal . . .

BARDOLPH

Regard me as your servant!
I am Bardolph and fervent.

PISTOL

I am Pistol and trusty.

FORD

Will you promise?

BARDOLPH

Our word is as good as gold . . .

PISTOL

. . . and even better.

FORD

Are we in agreement? On your honor?

Yes.   BARDOLPH, PISTOL

(The four women appear in the background)

DR. CAJUS *(to Ford)*

Even when of utmost gravity
A disease is often curable.
Nature's power will surprise you
And assist you when you're ill.
In a matter of depravity
That to you seems unendurable
As a doctor I advise you:
Hold your nose and take a pill!

PISTOL *(to Ford)*

One good way to make him pliable
Is to flatter his cupidity.
You remember what I told you
Of his liking for liquidity.
For it is quite undeniable:
Wine will quickly make him fall.
In his arms he will enfold you
And at last will tell you all.

FORD *(to Pistol)*

You will see my virtuosity
In the way I shall ensnare him,
Then the tigerish ferocity
I'll display when I shall tear him.
The old rascal will be sorry
For my vengeance cannot fail
When the hunter turns to quarry
And the snake will bite its tail!

BARDOLPH *(to Ford)*

Master Ford, you must be drastic
For this case is most precarious:
With your wife a total stranger
Who will surely go too far!
Yes, I know it seems fantastic,
But that drunkard is nefarious.
You will run a fatal danger
Leaving matters as they are.

FENTON *(to himself)*

Ah, these men and all this blabbering
They are planning and are scheming,
Over there the women jabbering
How did all this clamor start?
There I see her, sweet and beautiful
Her, whose love is mine forever,
Like a star come down from Heaven.
She will always hold my heart.

ALICE *(to Meg)*

Watch out, you polygamist
Disguised as a vat,
The fate of a bigamist
Is sad when you're fat!

MEG *(to Alice)*

Your shameless duplicity,
You monster, you rat,
Will bring you publicity,
We'll wager on that!

ANN *(to Alice)*

You symbol of vanity,
You lecher, you gnat,
We'll bring you to sanity,
And hand you your hat.

QUICKLY

For all his fatuity
He's quick as a cat:
'Twill take ingenuity
To batter him flat.

(All the men exit.)

ALICE
Qui più non si vagoli...

NANNETTA (a Quickly)
Tu corri all'ufficio tuo.

ALICE
Vo' ch'egli miagoli d'amore come un
Micio.
                    (a Quickly)
È intesa.

QUICKLY
Sì.

NANNETTA
È detta.

ALICE
Domani.

QUICKLY
Sì. Sì.

ALICE
Buon dì, Meg.

QUICKLY
Nannetta, Buon dì.

NANNETTA
Addio.

MEG
Buon dì.

ALICE
(trattenendo ancora le altre)
Vedrai che quell'epa terribile e tronfia
Si gonfia.

ALICE, NANNETTA
Si gonfia.

ALICE, MEG, QUICKLY E NANNETTA
Si gonfia e poi crepa.

ALICE
«Ma il viso mio su lui risplendrà . . .»

TUTTE
Come una stella sull'immensita!.
Ha, ha, ha, ha!
(Si accomiatano e s'allontanano
ridendo.)

ATTO SECONDO
PARTE PRIMA

L'interno dell'Osteria della Giarrettiera,
come nell'atto primo.

Falstaff sempre adagiato nel suo gran
seggiolone al suo solito posto bevendo
il suo Xeres. Bardolfo e Pistola verso
il fondo accanto all porta di sinistra.

BARDOLFO, PISTOLA
(Cantando insieme e battendosi il petto
in atto di pentimento)
Siam pentiti e contriti.

FALSTAFF
(volgendosi appena verso Bardolfo e
Pistola)
L'uomo ritorna al vizio, la gatta al
Lardo . . .

BARDOLEO, PISTOLA
E noi, torniamo al tuo servizio.

BARDOLFO (a Falstaff)
Pardon, là c'è una donna che alla
Vostra presenza
Chiede d'essere ammessa.

FALSTAFF
S'inoltri.
(Bardolfo esce da sinistra e ritorna
subito accompagnando Mrs.
Quickly.)

QUICKLY
(inchinandosi profondamente verso
Falstaff il quale è ancora seduto)
Reverenza!

FALSTAFF
Buon giorno, buona donna.

QUICKLY
Se Vostra Grazia vuole,
(avvicinandosi con gran rispetto e
cautela)
Vorrei, segretamente,
Dirle quattro parole.

FALSTAFF
T'accordo udienza.
(a Bardolfo e Pistola, rimasti nel fondo
a spiare)
Escite.
(Escono da sinistra facendo sberleffi.)

QUICKLY
(facendo un altro inchino ed avvicinandosi più di prima)
Reverenza! Madonna Alice Ford...

ALICE
Enough of this jabbering!

ANN (*to Quickly*)
'Tis time now for you to go.

ALICE
He shall be howling like a cat in the
  moonlight.
        (*to Quickly*)
You follow?

QUICKLY
Yes.

ANN
That's splendid.

ALICE
Tomorrow!

QUICKLY
Yes! Yes!

ALICE
Good day, Meg.

QUICKLY
My Annie, good day!

ANN
Good day.

MEG
Good day.

ANN
Good day.

MEG
Good day.

ALICE
(*holding the others back*)
We'll see how his belly will soon be ex-
  panding, and growing . . .

ALICE, ANN
. . . and bloating . . .

ALICE, ANN, MEG
. . . and growing. . . .

ALL FOUR WOMEN
. . . and bloating until it bursts!

ALICE
"Your radiant beauty on me will shed
  its light. . . ."

ALICE, ANN
". . . as bright and smiling . . ."

ALL
". . . out of the sky a star will shine at
  night!" Ha, ha, ha, ha!

(*They all leave laughing.*)

ACT TWO

PART ONE

(*At the Garter Inn, as in Act One.
Falstaff again seated in his armchair,
drinking his sherry. Bardolph and
Pistol near the door to the left.*)

BARDOLPH, PISTOL
(*singing together and beating their
chests in a gesture of contrition*)
See us sighing, weak from crying!

FALSTAFF
(*barely turning towards Bardolph and
Pistol*)
Men will return to vice like mice to the
  larder.

BARDOLPH, PISTOL
Let us return once more to serve you!

BARDOLPH (*to Falstaff*)
Outside the door there's someone waiting . . .
A woman who would like you to see
  her.

FALSTAFF
I'll see her.
(*Bardolph exits to the left and returns
at once with Mrs. Quickly.*)

QUICKLY
(*curtsying deeply towards Falstaff who
remains seated*)
I am honored.

FALSTAFF
Advance, my worthy woman!

QUICKLY
I am honored. Sir John, with your per-
  mission
        (*advancing cautiously*)
I shall, but most discreetly,
Submit a proposition.

FALSTAFF
Your wish be granted.
(*to Bardolph and Pistol who have re-
mained in the background to listen*)
Pray, leave us!
(*The two leave, showing their dis-
appointment.*)

QUICKLY
(*curtsies again, then draws nearer to
Falstaff*)
I am honored. You know a Mistress
Ford. . . .

FALSTAFF

(*alzandosi ed accostandosi a Quickly premuroso*)

Ebben?

QUICKLY

Ahimè! Povera donna! Siete un gran Seduttore!

FALSTAFF (*subito*)

Lo so. Continua.

QUICKLY

Alice sta in grande agitazione d'amor
Per voi; vi dice ch'ebbe la vostra lettera,
Che vi ringrazia e che suo marito esce
Sempre dalle due alle tre.

FALSTAFF

Dalle due alle tre.

QUICKLY

Vostra Grazia a quell'ora
Potrà liberamente salir dove dimora
La bella Alice. Povera donna! le angoscie sue
Son crudeli! ha un marito geloso!

FALSTAFF

(*rimuginando le parole di Quickly*)

Dalle due alle tre.

(*a Quickly*)

Le dirai che impaziente aspetto
Quell'ora. Al mio dovere non mancherò.

QUICKLY

Ben detto.
Ma c'è un'altra ambasciata per Vostra Grazia.

FALSTAFF

Parla.

QUICKLY

La bella Meg (un angelo che innamora a guardarla)
Anch'essa vi saluta molto amorosamente;
Dice che suo marito è assai di rado assente.
Povera donna! un giglio di candore e di fè!
Voi le stregate tutte.

FALSTAFF

Stregoneria non c'è
Ma un certo qual mio fascino personal . . .
Dimmi: l'altra sa di quest'altra?

QUICKLY

Oibò! La donna nasce scaltra. Non. temete.

FALSTAFF

(*cercando nella sua borsa*)

Or ti vo' remunerar . . .

QUICKLY

Chi semina grazie, raccoglie amore.

FALSTAFF

(*estraendo una moneta e porgendola a Quickly*)

Prendi, Mercurio-femina.

(*congedandola col gesto*)

Saluta le due dame.

QUICKLY

M'inchino. (*Esce.*)

(*Falstaff solo, poi Bardolfo, poi Mr. Ford, poi Pistola.*)

FALSTAFF

Alice è mia!

Va, vecchio John, va, va per la tua via.
Questa tua vecchia carne ancora spreme
Qualche dolcezza a te.
Tutte le donne ammutinate insieme
Si dannano per me!
Buon corpo di Sir John, ch'io nutro e sazio,
Va, ti ringrazio.

BARDOLFO

(*entrando da sinistra*)

Pardon, di là c'è un certo Messer Mastro Fontana
Che anela di conoscervi; offre una damigiana
Di Cipro per l'asciolvere di Vostra Signoria.

FALSTAFF

Il suo nome è Fontana?

BARDOLFO

Sì.

FALSTAFF

Bene accolta sia
La fontana che spande un simile liquore!
Entri. (*Bardolfo esce.*)
Va, vecchio John, per la tua via.

FALSTAFF

(*rises and turns towards Quickly, with an ambiguous smile, as if to say "Tell me more!"*)

I do . . . ?

QUICKLY

Alas! Unhappy woman! You're a brazen seducer. . . .

FALSTAFF

I know. Continue!

QUICKLY

The lady is raving with delirious passion for you.
Your letter fills her with love and gratitude.
This I should tell you. . . .
And that daily her husband is absent
From eleven to one.

FALSTAFF

From eleven to one!

QUICKLY

'Tis the time your Grace could meet her,
And free of danger venture
  in her own home to greet her.
What an adventure! Unhappy woman!
For what she suffers is inhuman:
Master Ford is a demon!

FALSTAFF

(*mulling over Quickly's remarks*)
. . . from eleven to one!

(*to Quickly*)

Go and tell her that my heart is waiting to see her.
My duty tells me what to do!

QUICKLY

I bless you.
There is still one more message I am to bring you. . . .

FALSTAFF

Tell me!

QUICKLY

This one from Meg—an angel whom to behold is to worship!
She, too, has asked me to assure you of her great ardor.
She has a spouse who all the time stays in the house to guard her. Unhappy woman!
As white as snow is her innocent heart!
No one escapes your magic.

FALSTAFF

I cast no magic spell.
And yet I wield a certain charm of my own.
Tell me: Each one keeps her own secret?

QUICKLY

Of course! No woman tells another . . . not in this case.

FALSTAFF

(*searching his purse*)

You have earned a just reward.

QUICKLY

Who soweth his favors shall harvest love.

FALSTAFF

(*offering her a small coin*)

Take this, you female Mercury!

(*dismissing her with a gesture*)

Be sure to greet my ladies!

QUICKLY

Your servant! (*Exits*)

(*Falstaff alone, later Bardolph, Ford, and Pistol*)

FALSTAFF

She's mine! I've won her!
Go, gallant John, go, go onward to glory!
You, mighty mound of matter, once more shall render
Your gen'rous help to me.
Women are haunted by your spacious splendor,
As anyone can see.
My paunch, at last I know why I should feed you.
Thanks! I shall need you.

BARDOLPH

(*entering from the left*)

Sir John, I have a message from a Master Brook
Who wants to have a word with you;
And he offers you a demijohn of Cyprus to assure you of a pleasant morning.

FALSTAFF

And this Brook, is he here now?

BARDOLPH

Yes.

FALSTAFF

I am fond of brooks that run so freely, whose flow bespeaks such tasty tidings.
He's welcome! (*Bardolph exits*)
Go, gallant John, onward to glory!

(Ford, travestito, entra da sinistra, preceduto da Bardolfo che si ferma all'uscio e s'inchina al suo passaggio e seguito da Pistola, il quale tiene una damigiana che depone sul tavolo. Pistola e Bardolfo restano nel fondo. Ford tiene un sacchetto in mano.)

FORD

(avanzandosi dopo un grande inchino a Falstaff)

Signore, v'assista il cielo!

FALSTAFF

(ricambiando il saluto)

Assista voi pur, signore.

FORD

(sempre complimentoso)

Io sono, davver, molto indiscreto,
E vi chiedo perdono,
Se, senza cerimonie, qui vengo e
 sprovveduto
Di più lunghi preamboli.

FALSTAFF

Voi siete il benvenuto.

FORD

In me vedete un uomo ch'ha
 un'abbondanza grande
Degli agi della vita; un uom che spende
 e spande
Come più gli talenta pur di passar
 mattana.
Io mi chiamo Fontana!

FALSTAFF

(andando a stringergli la mano con grande cordialità)

Caro signor Fontana!
Voglio fare con voi più ampia
 conoscenza.

FORD

Caro Sir John, desidero parlarvi in
 confidenza.

BARDOLFO

(sottovoce a Pistola nel fondo, spiando)

Attento!

PISTOLA

(sottovoce a Bardolfo)

Zitto!

BARDOLFO

Guarda! Scommetto! Egli va dritto
Nel trabocchetto.

PISTOLA

Ford se lo intrappola . . .

BARDOLFO

Zitto!

FALSTAFF

(a Bardolfo e Pistola, i quali escono al cenno di Falstaff)

Che fate là?

(a Ford, col quale è rimasto solo)

V'ascolto.

FORD

Sir John, m'infonde ardire
Un ben noto proverbio popolar: si suol
 dire
Che l'oro apre ogni porta, che l'oro è
 un talismano,
Che l'oro vince tutto.

FALSTAFF

L'oro è un buon capitano che marcia
 avanti.

FORD

(avviandosi verso il tavolo)

Ebbene. Ho un sacco di monete
Qua, che mi pesa assai. Sir John, se voi
 volete
Aiutarmi a portarlo . . .

FALSTAFF

(prende il sacchetto e lo depone sul tavolo.)

Con gran piacer . . . non so,
Davver, per qual mio merito,
Messer . . .

FORD

Ve lo dirò.
C'è a Windsor una dama, bella e
 leggiadra molto.
Si chiama Alice; è moglie d'un certo
 Ford.

FALSTAFF

V'ascolto.

FORD

Io l'amo e lei non m'ama; le scrivo,
 non risponde;
La guardo, non mi guarda; la cerco e
 si nasconde.
Per lei sprecai tesori, gittai doni su
 doni,
Escogitai, tremando, il vol delle
 occasioni.
Ahimè! tutto fu vano! Rimasi sulle
 scale,
Negletto, a bocca asciutta, cantando un
 madrigale.

FALSTAFF

(canterellando scherzosamente)

L'amor, l'amor che non ci dà mai
 tregue
Finchè la vita strugge
È come l'ombra . . .

(Ford enters in disguise from the left, preceded by Bardolph who stays near the entrance and bows as Ford passes. The latter is followed by Pistol who carries a demijohn which he sets on the table. Pistol and Bardolph remain in the background. Ford is holding a bag of money.)

FORD

(after bowing low)
Your Worship, may Heaven bless you!

FALSTAFF

(returning the greeting)
His Mercy may be on you, Sir!

FORD *(respectfully)*

As I am aware, my bold intrusion—with your kindly forebearance—seems to be quite ill-mannered, an insolent presumption, as a gentleman ought to know.

FALSTAFF

You could not be more welcome!

FORD

In me you see a man who lives in wealth and bounty,
Whose every wish is granted—
A man who lends and spends and never cared, never counted.
Sir, I shall no longer bore you:
Master Brook stands before you.

FALSTAFF

(shaking his hand most cordially)
Good Master Brook, I greet you.
From the first you have made a most profound impression.

FORD

Gallant Sir John, I trust I may have faith in your discretion.

BARDOLPH

(whispering to Pistol, both hiding in the background)
Attention!

PISTOL

(softly to Bardolph)
Quiet!

BARDOLPH

Watch it! How wily!
You can't deny it . . . he does it slyly!

PISTOL

Netting the butterfly!

BARDOLPH

Quiet!

FALSTAFF

(to Bardolph and Pistol who subsequently disappear)
Are you still here?
(to Ford who remains alone with him)
Continue!

FORD

Sir John, will you allow me to resort to a wise and ancient saw: "When the key is of gold, no lock will resist it."?

To gold and all its splendor,
To gold they all surrender.

FALSTAFF

Gold will conquer the world, proudly marching onward.

FORD

Precisely! Perchance I find this bag of gold weighs too much for me. Sir John, may I impose upon your kindness to help me?

FALSTAFF

(taking the bag and placing it on the table)
Of course I shall!
But may I know why it is I whom you have chosen. . . .

FORD

You may indeed.
In Windsor lives a lady, lovely, demure, and haunting.
Her name is Alice, her husband a certain Ford.

FALSTAFF

Enchanting.

FORD

I woo her . . . cannot subdue her,
Implore her . . . seem to bore her,
Beseech her . . . cannot reach her,
Pursue her . . . cannot get to her!
In desperate delusion,
to show that I adore her,
In unrestrained profusion
I spread my wealth before her.
Alas . . . all this was useless!
A castaway crusader,
I flounder and fly around her,
And sadly serenade her!

FALSTAFF *(gaily)*

I know, I know that love is blessed and blighted, how love will twit and taunt you, and like a shadow . . .

FORD

. . . Che chi fugge . . .

FALSTAFF

. . . insegue . . .

FORD

E chi l'insegue . . .

FALSTAFF

. . . fugge . . .

FORD

E questo madrigale l'ho appreso a prezzo d'ôr.

FALSTAFF

Quest'è il destin fatale del misero amator.
Essa non vi die' mai luogo a lusinghe?

FORD

No.

FALSTAFF

Ma infin, perchè v'aprite a me?

FORD

Ve lo dirò:
Voi siete un gentiluomo prode, arguto, facondo,
Voi siete un uom di guerra, voi siete un uom di mondo . . .

FALSTAFF (*con gesto d'umiltà*)

Oh! . . .

FORD

Non vi adulo, e quello è un sacco di monete:
Spendetele! spendetele! sì, spendete e spandete
Tutto il mio patrimonio! Siate ricco e felice!
Ma, in contraccambio, chiedo che conquistiate Alice!

FALSTAFF

Strana ingiunzion!

FORD

Mi spiego: Quella crudel beltà
Sempre è vissuta in grande fede di castità.
La sua virtù importuna m'abbarbagliava gli occhi:
La bella inespugnabile dicea: Guai se mi tocchi.
Ma se voi l'espugnate, poi, posso anch'io sperar:
Da fallo nasce fallo e allor . . . Che ve ne par?

FALSTAFF

Prima di tutto, senza complimenti, Messere,
Accetto il sacco. E poi (fede di cavaliere,
Qua la mano!) farò le vostre brame sazie.

(*stringendo forte la mano a Ford*)

Voi, la moglie di Ford possederete.

FORD

Grazie!!

FALSTAFF

Io son già molto innanzi; (non c'è ragion ch'io taccia
Con voi) fra una mezz'ora sarà nelle mie braccia.

FORD (*come un urlo*)

Chi? . . .

FALSTAFF (*con calma*)

Alice. Essa mandò dianzi una . . . confidente
Per dirmi che quel tanghero di suo marito è assente
Dalle due alle tre.

FORD

Dalle due alle tre . . .
Lo conoscete?

FALSTAFF

Il diavolo
Se lo porti all'inferno con Menelao suo avolo! Quel tanghero,
Vedrai! Te lo cornifico netto! se mi frastorna
Gli sparo una girandola di botte sulle corna!

FORD

. . . it will haunt you . . .

FALSTAFF

. . . you fight it . . .

FORD

. . . and as you fight it . . .

FALSTAFF

'twill haunt you!

FORD

You know . . .

FALSTAFF

. . . quite so . . .

FORD

. . . my woe . . .

FALSTAFF

. . . I know!

FORD

To suffer and to languish
  I've paid my weight in gold.

FALSTAFF

The amatory anguish
  will torture young and old!
And not even once she seemed to be
  yielding?

FORD

No.

FALSTAFF

But why pour out your heart to me?

FORD

Let me explain:
You are a man of bearing, noble, well-
  spoken, and cunning,
A man of fearless daring whose gallant-
  ry is stunning.

FALSTAFF (*humbly*)

. . . well . . .

FORD

I am serious. My gold shall serve to
  make you happy:
Away with it! Go play with it!
  You shall spend and expend it,
You shall cherish and befriend it,
  you shall live in its splendor!
All I am asking
  is that to you she must surrender.

FALSTAFF

What do you mean?

FORD

Quite simply:
My lovely iceberg prides herself
On being thought a paragon of chastity.
Her virtuous demeanor
  has made my passion keener.
Her eyes will tell the world for all to
  see:
"No one come near me!"
But if you, Sir, should win her,
I, in due time, may, too:
One fall makes her a sinner . . .
  and then . . . is this not true?

FALSTAFF

Now to begin and expedite the matter
I shall accept your money. Then (here
  is my hand upon it) . . .
You may trust me! your pain and
  trouble shall be ended.
  (*shaking Ford's hand*)
You shall win Mistress Ford . . . she will
  surrender!

FORD

Splendid!

FALSTAFF

I'm well along my way, Sir,
(Why should I hide my secret from
  you?)
This very day, Sir, I swear I shall embrace her!

FORD

(*surprised, half choking*)

Whom?

FALSTAFF (*calmly*)

Your Alice. Someone she sent to me this
  morning has told me that the simpleton she calls a husband is absent from
  eleven to one.

FORD (*sourly*)

Pray, do you know him?

FALSTAFF

For all I care he may simmer in Hell
  and choke on his own stupidity!
That simpleton, that addle-head,
The scamp, the fool, the lout,
I'll cast him out,
make him horniferous, neatly, sweetly!
Should he be mulish
I'll show him how to crown his brow
  and even seem more foolish!
Ford is a cow, a bullock!
He's mooing and chewing and booing.
Watch out how I shall twit him!
No doubt I shall outwit him.

Quel Messer Ford è un bue! Un bue!
Te lo corbello,

Vedrai! Ma è tardi. Aspettami qua.
Vado a farmi bello.

(*Piglia il sacco di monete ed esce dal
fondo. Mr. Ford solo*)

FORD

È sogno? o realtà? . . . Due rami enormi

Crescon sulla mia testa.

È un sogno? Mastro Ford! Mastro
Ford! Dormi?

Svegliati! Su! ti desta!

Tua moglie sgarra e mette in mal'
assetto

L'onor tuo, la tua casa ed il tuo letto!

L'ora è fissata, tramato l'inganno;

Sei gabbato e truffato! . . .

E poi diranno

Che un marito geloso è un insensato!

Già dietro a me nomi d'infame conio

Fischian passando; mormora lo scherno.

O matrimonio: Inferno!

Donna: Demonio!

Nella lor moglie abbian fede i babbei!

Affiderei

La mia birra a un Tedesco,

Tutto il mio desco

A un Olandese lurco,

La mia bottiglia d'acquavite a un
Turco,

Non mia moglie a se stessa. O laida
sorte!

Quella brutta parola in cor mi torna:

Le corna! Bue! capron! le fusa torte!

Ah! le corna! le corna!

Ma non mi sfuggirai! no! sozzo, reo,

Dannato epicureo!

Prima li accoppio

E poi li colgo. Io scoppio!

Vendicherò l'affronto!

Laudata sempre sia

Nel fondo del mio cor la gelosia.

FALSTAFF

(*rientrando dalla porta del fondo. Ha
un farsetto nuovo, cappello e
bastone.*)

Eccomi qua. Son pronto.
M'accompagnate un tratto?

FORD

Vi metto sulla via.

(*Si avviano: giunti presso alla soglia
fanno dei gesti complimentosi per
cedere la precedenza del passo.*)

FALSTAFF

Prima voi.

FORD

Prima voi.

FALSTAFF

No. Sono in casa mia.
Passate.

FORD

Prego . . .

FALSTAFF

È tardi. L'appuntamento preme.

FORD

Non fate complimenti . . .

FALSTAFF

Ebben, passiamo insìeme.

(*Prende il braccio di Ford sotto il suo
ed escono a braccetto.*)

PARTE SECONDA

(*Una sala nella casa di Ford.*

*Amphia finestra nel fondo. Porto a
destra, porta a sinistra e un'altra
porta verso l'angolo di destra nel
fondo che esce sulla scala. Un'altra
scala nell'angolo del fondo a sinistra.
Dal gran finestrone spalancato si
vede il giardino. Un paravento chiuso
sta appoggiato alla parete di sinistra,
accanto ad un vasto camino. Armadio
addosso alla parete di destra. Un
tavolino, una cassapanca. Lungo le
pareti, un seggiolone e qualche scran-
no. Sul seggiolone, un liuto. Sul tavolo, dei fiori.*

*Alice, Meg poi Quickly dalla porta a
destra ridendo. Poi Nanetta.*)

The lout, I clout his snout,
Make him horniferous, neatly, sweetly.
That simpleton, I'll better him,
that vagabond, I'll fetter him!
You wait here until I return,
harnessed in grace and beauty!

(*Falstaff takes the bag of money and
exits through the door in the back.
Ford remains alone.*)

FORD

A nightmare . . . an evil dream? A
monstrous fork is growing out of my
forehead!

A nightmare? Master Ford, Master
Ford . . . awaken, rouse yourself, look
and listen!

Your wife is straying . . . her scandal-
ous flirtation
Will go on to adult'ry and degradation!
Planned with affection and timed to
perfection!
Go and try to prevent it! And yet they'll
tell me
That a man who is jealous is demented!
All over town I hear them taunt and
jeer me,
Whisp'ring their insults, whistling when
they're near me.
Marriage is treason infernal,
Torment eternal!
Ah, what a fool, he who trusts in a
woman!
I should entrust my champagne to a
Frenchman
Or ask a Dutchman to patrol my
pantry,
I'd trust a scoundrel without name or
gentry
But no wife and her virtue! Oh fright,
oh sorrow!
I remember the words he spoke to warn
me:
"The horns, Sir!" Horror . . . 'tis true
. . .
Maybe tomorrow . . . Ah, they're grow-
ing, they're showing!
Ah, I will take revenge! You sniper . . .
swiper . . .
You Godforsaken viper!
First I'll abet them, then I shall fret
them,
Beset them, and net them . . .
Abet them, then fret, beset them and
get them and finally net them
Yes, net them!
I shall avenge my honor!
Come triumph or perdition,

I thank my guiding star for my
suspicion!

(*Falstaff returns through the door in
the background, dressed up in a new
vest, wearing a hat and carrying a
cane.*)

FALSTAFF

Shall we proceed? I'm ready.
You'll take me on my way, Sir?

FORD

I could not bear to stay, Sir.

(*They start to leave. Near the door they
stop, each one motioning to the other
to be the first to leave.*)

FALSTAFF

If you please . . .

FORD

After you. . . .

FALSTAFF

No, no! You're my guest, remember!
I pray you!

FORD

You first!

FALSTAFF

A lady should never be kept waiting.

FORD

On this there's no debating.

FALSTAFF

I beg you . . .

FORD

Please, Sir!

FALSTAFF

Well then . . . two friends united!

(*They leave together, arm in arm.*)

PART TWO

A room in Ford's house.

*A large window in the back through
which we look out into the garden.
Two doors, one to the left and one to
the right. A third door leading to the
stairway in the background, to the
right. A folded screen leaning against
the wall to the left, near a large fire-
place. A cupboard on the right. A
small table. A chest. Along the walls
an armchair and several other chairs.
On the armchair a lute. Flowers on
the table.*

(*Alice, Meg, later Quickly entering
from the door to the right. Later
Ann.*)

ALICE

Presenteremo un bill, per una tassa
Al parlamento, sulla gente grassa.

QUICKLY (*entrando*)

Comari!

ALICE

(*accorrendo con Meg verso Quickly,
mentre Nannetta ch'è entrata anch'
essa resta triste in disparte*)

Ebben?

MEG

Che c'è?

QUICKLY

Sarà sconfitto!

ALICE

Brava!

QUICKLY

Fra poco gli farem la festa!

ALICE, MEG

Bene!

QUICKLY

Piombò nel laccio a capo fitto.

ALICE

Narrami tutto, lesta.

MEG

Lesta.

ALICE

Lesta.

QUICKLY

Giunta all'Albergo della Giarrettiera
Chiedo d'essere ammessa alla presenza
Del Cavalier, segreta messaggera.
Sir John si degna d'accordarmi udienza,
M'accoglie tronfio in furfantesca posa:
«Buon giorno, buona donna.»
«Reverenza.»
A lui m'inchino molto ossequïosa-
-mente, poi passo alle notizie ghiotte.
Lui beve grosso ed ogni mia massiccia
Frottola inghiotte.
Infin, per farla spiccia,
Vi crede entrambe innamorate cotte
Delle bellezze sue.
E lo vedrete presto ai vostri piè.

ALICE

Quando?

QUICKLY

Oggi, qui, dalle due alle tre.

MEG

Dalle due alle tre.

ALICE

(*guardando l'oriolo*)

Son già le due.

(*correndo subito all'uscio del fondo e
chiamando*)

Olà! Ned! Will!

(*a Quickly*)

Già tutto ho preparato.

(*Torna a gridare dall'uscio verso
l'esterno.*)

Portate qui la cesta del bucato.

QUICKLY

Sarà un affare gaio!

ALICE (*a Nannetta*)

Nannetta, e tu non ridi? Che cos'hai?
Tu piangi? Che cos'hai? Dillo a tua
madre.

NANNETTA (*singhiozzando*)

Mio padre . . .

ALICE

Ebben?

NANNETTA

Mio padre . . .

ALICE

Ebben?

NANNETTA

Mio padre . . . (*scoppiando in lagrime*)
Vuole ch'io mi mariti al Dottor Cajo!!

ALICE

A quel pedante?!

QUICKLY

Oibò!

MEG

A quel gonzo!

ALICE

A quel grullo!

NANNETTA

A quel bisavolo!

ALICE

No! No!

MEG, QUICKLY

No! No!

TUTTE

No! No!

NANNETTA

Piuttosto lapidata viva . . .

ALICE

Da una mitraglia di torsi di cavolo.

ALICE

A bill we'll send to Parliament will shortly set a tax on people fat and portly.

QUICKLY *(entering)*

My ladies!

ALICE

(running towards her, as does Meg, while Ann, entering simultaneously, stays aside, obviously unhappy.)

So soon?

MEG

The news?

QUICKLY

. . . could not be better!

ALICE

Really?

QUICKLY

Our gallant knight will be unseated . . .

ALICE, MEG

Splendid!

QUICKLY

. . . Sir Falstaff utterly defeated!

ALICE

What happened? Come and tell us!

QUICKLY

Stepping inside the "Garter" Inn to greet him
I conveyed my respects, only to mention
That I was sent by someone else to meet him.
Sir John at once lent me his kind attention.
His welcome truly bespoke his vast dimension:
"Advance, my worthy woman" . . . "I am honored".
I curtsied deeply in my most obsequious manner.
Then I proceeded to ensnare him, a willing victim.
I saw him pick and lick the candystick I gave him.
In short, Sir Falstaff's haughtiness
Is certain of your naughtiness
And sure that for his beauty
You will forget your duty.
So be prepared to see him at your knees this very day!

ALICE

Heavens!

QUICKLY

Surely! Now . . . from eleven to one!

MEG

From eleven to one?

ALICE

(looking at the clock)

'T is now eleven.

(hurrying to the door and calling outside)

Come here, Ned! Will!

(to Quickly)

I've cleared the deck for action.

(calling back to the outside)

Bring in the basket ready for the laundry!

QUICKLY

We'll drive him to distraction.

ALICE *(to Ann)*

My goodness! You are so serious. Tell me why!
You're weeping. Tell me why! Come, tell your mother!

ANN *(sobbing)*

My father. . . .

ALICE

Go on!

ANN

My father . . .

ALICE

Speak up!

ANN

My father . . . *(breaking out in tears)* told me
That I should marry Doctor Cajus!

ALICE

That dodd'ring dandy?

QUICKLY

Good Lord!

MEG

That old pillbox?

ALICE

. . . scabby millfox?

ANN

. . . so thin and underweight!

ALL

No! No!

ANN

I'd rather drown or die of fever!

ALICE

. . . or be shot dead by a volley of pomegranate!

QUICKLY

Ben detto!

MEG

Brava!

ALICE

Non temer.

NANNETTA

(saltando di gioia)

Evviva!
Col Dottor Cajo non mi sposerò!

(Intanto entrano due servi portando
una cesta piena di biancheria.)

ALICE (ai servi)

Mettete là. Poi, quando avrò chiamato,
Vuoterete la cesta nel fossato.

NANNETTA

Bum!

ALICE

(a Nannetta, poi ai servi che escono)

Taci. Andate.

NANNETTA

Che bombardamento!

ALICE

Prepariamo la scena.

(Corre a pigliare una sedia e la mette
presso al tavolo.)

Qua una sedia.

NANNETTA

(Corre a pigliare il liuto e lo mette
sulla tavola.)

Qua il mio liuto.

ALICE

Apriamo il paravento.

(Nannetta e Meg corrono a prendere
il paravento, lo aprono dopo averlo
collocato fra la cesta e il camino.)

Bravissime! Così. Più aperto ancora.
Fra poco s'incomincia la commedia,
Gaie comari di Windsor! è l'ora!
L'ora d'alzar la risata sonora!
L'alta risata che scoppia, che scherza,
Che sfolgora, armata
Di dardi e di sferza!
Gaie comari! festosa brigata!

Sul lieto viso
Spunti il sorriso,
Splenda del riso l'acuto fulgor!
Favilla incendiaria
Di gioia nell'aria,
Di gioia nel cor.

(a Meg)

A noi! - Tu la parte farai che ti spetta.

MEG (ad Alice)

Tu corri il tuo rischio col grosso
compar.

QUICKLY

Is sto alla vedetta.

ALICE (a Quickly)

Se sbagli ti fischio.

NANNETTA

Io resto in disparte sull'uscio a spiar.

ALICE

E mostreremo all'uom che l'allegria
D'oneste donne ogni onestà comporta.
Fra le femine quella è la più ria
Che fa la gattamorta.

QUICKLY

(che sarà andata alla finestra)

Eccolo! È lui!

ALICE

Dov'è?

QUICKLY

Poco discosto.

NANNETTA

Presto.

QUICKLY

A salir s'avvia.

ALICE

(Prima a Nanetta indica l'uscio a sinistra: poi a Meg, indicando l'uscio di
destra.)

Tu di qua. Tu di là

NANNETTA

(Esce correndo da sinistra,)

Al posto!

MEG

(Esce correndo da destra con Quickly.)

Al posto!

QUICKLY

No question!

MEG

Really!

ALICE

Have no fear!

ANN

(*jumping with joy*)

Ah, thank you!

Dear Doctor Cajus, my reply is No!

(*Two servants have brought a basket filled with linen and other objects to be laundered.*)

ALICE (*to the servants*)

Put it down here. As soon as I shall call you, you will empty the basket into the river.

ANN

Splash!

ALICE

(*to Ann, then to the servants about to leave*)

Quiet! Be ready!

ANN

What a mighty tumble!

ALICE

Let's prepare the arena!

(*picks up a chair and sets it near the table*)

Here the chair.

ANN

(*bringing the lute from the armchair and putting it on the table*)

Here my lute!

ALICE

The screen we better open.

(*Ann and Meg open the screen and place it between the basket and the fire-place.*)

Just put it there . . . like this! A little wider! The stage is set, the comedy has started.

Merrily pulling the curtain, we greet you,

Meet you with smiles and most gaily entreat you:

Join in the folly and frolic and banter

We'll pour on that jolly and foolish enchanter!

See how we beat him with lances of laughter,

See how we cheat him, how we defeat him,

How we delete him and tear him apart!

Yet all that is done

Will only be fun

And make all of us happy in mind and in heart.

(*to Meg*)

But now . . . You will know what to do . . . are you certain?

MEG (*to Alice*)

You're taking your chances with mighty Sir John.

QUICKLY

I'll stay at the curtain.

ALICE (*to Quickly*)

. . . and watch his advances!

ANN

And I'd better go, but be sure I'll look on!

ALICE

Now let us show our husbands so imperious

That fun and folly need not disgrace a lady.

When a woman pretends to be too serious

She's likely to be shady!

QUICKLY

Quiet now! He's here.

ALICE

But where?

QUICKLY

Right near the entrance.

ANN

Hurry!

QUICKLY

He is in the doorway.

ALICE

(*first motioning Ann to leave to the left, then to Meg to leave to the right*)

You go there! And you there! Your places!

ANN

(*running off to the left*)

Let's hurry!

MEG

(*running off to the right*)

Our places!

QUICKLY

Al posto!

(*Alice sola. Poi Falstaff. Alice si sarà accanto al tavolo, avrà preso il liuto toccando qualche accordo.*)

FALSTAFF

(*Entra con vivacità; vedendola suonare, si mette a cantarellare.*)

Alfin t'ho colto, raggiante fior, T'ho colto!

(*Prende Alice pel busto. Alice avrà cessato di suonare e si sarà alzata.*)

Ed or potrò morir felice.
Avrò vissuto molto dopo quest'ora di beato amor.

ALICE

O soave sir John!

FALSTAFF

Mia bella Alice!
Non so far lo svenevole,
Nè lusingar, nè usar frase fiorita,
Ma dirò tosto un mio pensier colpevole.

ALICE

Cioè?

FALSTAFF

Cioè: Vorrei che Mastro Ford
Passasse a miglior vita . . .

ALICE

Perchè?

FALSTAFF

Perchè? Lo chiedi?
Saresti la mia Lady e Falstaff il tuo Lord.

ALICE

Povera Lady inver!

FALSTAFF

Degna d'un Re.
T'immagino fregiata del mio stemma,
Mostrar fra gemma e gemma
La pompa del tuo sen.
Nell'iri ardente e mobile dei rai
Dell'adamante,
Col picciol piè nel nobile
Cerchio d'un guardinfante
Risplenderai
Più fulgida d'un ampio arcobalen.

ALICE

Ogni più bel gioiel mi nuoce e spregio
Il finto idolo d'or.
Mi basta un vel legato in croce, un fregio
Al cinto e in testa un fior.

(*Si mette un fiore nei capelli.*)

FALSTAFF
(*per abbracciarla*)

Sirena!

ALICE

(*facendo un passo indietro*)

Adulator!

FALSTAFF

Soli noi siamo
E non temiamo agguato.

ALICE

Ebben?

FALSTAFF

Io t'amo!

ALICE

(*scostandosi un poco*)

Voi siete nel peccato!

FALSTAFF (*avvicinandola*)

Sempre l'amor l'occasione azzecca.

ALICE

Sir John!

FALSTAFF

Chi segue vocazion non pecca.
T'amo! e non è mia colpa . . .

ALICE (*interrompendolo*)

Se tanta avete vulnerabil polpa . . .

FALSTAFF

Quand'ero paggio
Del Duca di Norfolk ero sottile,
Ero un miraggio
Vago, leggero, gentile, gentile.
Quello era il tempo del mio verde Aprile,
Quello era il tempo del mio lieto Maggio.
Tant'era smilzo, flessibile e snello
Che sarei guizzato attraverso un anello.

ALICE

Voi mi celiate.
Io temo i vostri inganni.
Temo che amiate . . .

QUICKLY

(*running off towards the rear*)

Let's hurry!

(*Alice alone. Later Falstaff. Alice sits near the table, playing some chords on the lute.*)

FALSTAFF

(*entering rapidly. Seeing her play the lute, he starts singing:*)

"I broke you, blossom so fair, so dear! I broke you!"

(*He tries to embrace Alice who stops playing and rises.*)

Come, King of Death, I now ignore you:

For paradise has opened in the enchantment of supreme delight!

ALICE

Oh, my charming Sir John!

FALSTAFF

How I adore you!
I am not made for jollity,
I cannot spin such fine, flowery phrases.
But I'll reveal to you an odd frivolity:

ALICE

How so?

FALSTAFF

I wish . . . I wish that Master Ford should rest beneath the daisies!

ALICE

And why?

FALSTAFF

And why? You ask me?
Then you could be my lady, and I could be your lord.

ALICE

I am too plain, I fear!

FALSTAFF

Fit for a king!
My coat-of-arms, ennobled by your beauty,
Will shine anew when worn by you on your heaving heart!
Your eyes will steal the milky glow
Of pearls craving to grace you,
Your bosom feel the silky flow
Of gowns eager to enlace you.
The stars on high will not deny
Your throne up in the sky!

ALICE

In all this splendor you might scorn me,
A woman much too humble for you.
Oh let your tenderness adorn me!
Instead of furbelows a rose will do.

(*puts a flower into her hair.*)

FALSTAFF

(*trying to embrace her*)

Enchantress!

ALICE

(*taking a step away from him*)

Oh please, Sir John!

FALSTAFF

You are with me, and no one will surprise you.

ALICE

You mean . . .?

FALSTAFF

I love you!

ALICE

(*keeping her distance from him*)

Your conscience will despise you.

FALSTAFF (*following her*)

My conscience tells me of our hearts' attraction.

ALICE

Sir John!

FALSTAFF

. . . compels me to pursue my action!
Passion never needs excuses . . .

ALICE (*cutting him short*)

. . . not even when it prompts severe abuses?

FALSTAFF

Once when in Norfolk in service to the Duke—
I was a page then, vivacious and tender,
I was a swain as light as the rain,
I was slight then and slender, yes, slender!
May of my youth so full of love and rapture,
Day that in truth I wish I could recapture!
I was as swift and slick as a sparrow,
Nimble as a deer and as quick as an arrow.

ALICE

You really charm me! And yet I know you'll harm me.
I have a rival!

FALSTAFF

Chi?

ALICE

Meg.

FALSTAFF

Colei? M'è in uggia la sua faccia.

ALICE

Non traditemi, John . . .

FALSTAFF

Mi par mill'anni
D'averti fra le braccia. T'amo . . .
(*rincorrendola e tentando d'abbracciarla*)

ALICE (*difendendosi*)

Per carità . . .

FALSTAFF

(*La prende attraverso il busto.*)
Vieni!

QUICKLY

(*dall'antisala gridando*)
Signora Alice!

FALSTAFF

(*Abbandona Alice e rimane turbato.*)
Chi va là?

QUICKLY

(*entrando e fingendo agitazione*)
Signora Alice!

ALICE

Che c'è?

QUICKLY

(*rapidamente ed interrotta dalla foga*)
Mia signora! C'è Mistress Meg
E vuol parlarvi, sbuffa . . . Strepita,
s'abbaruffa . . .

FALSTAFF

Alla malora!

QUICKLY

E vuol passar e la trattengo a stento . . .

FALSTAFF

Dove m'ascondo?

ALICE

Dietro il paravento.

(*Falstaff si rimpiatta dietro il paravento. Quando Falstaff è nascosto,
Quickly fa cenno a Meg che sta
dietro l'uscio di destra: Meg entra
fingendo d'essere agitatissima. Quickly torna ad uscire.*)

MEG

Alice! che spavento! Che chiasso!
Che discordia!
Non perdere un momento. Fuggi! . . .

ALICE

Misericordia! Che avvenne?

MEG

Il tuo consorte vien gridando
«accorr' uomo!»
Dice . . .

ALICE

(*presto a bassa voce*)
Parla più forte.

MEG

Che vuol scannare un uomo!

ALICE (*come sopra*)

Non ridere.

MEG

Ei correva invaso da tremendo
Furor! Maledicendo tutte le figlie
d'Eva!

ALICE

Misericordia!

MEG

Dice che un tuo ganzo hai nascosto;
Lo vuole ad ogni costo scoprir . . .

QUICKLY

(*ritornando spaventatissima e gridando
più di prima*)

Signora Alice! Vien Mastro Ford! Sal-
vatevi!
È come una tempesta!
Strepita, tuona, fulmina,
Si dà dei pugni in testa,
Scoppia in minaccie ed urla . . .

ALICE

(*avvicinandosi a Quickly a bassa voce
e un poco allarmata*)

Dassenno oppur da burla?

QUICKLY

(*ancora ad alta voce*)

Dassenno. Egli scavalca
Le siepi del giardino . . .
Lo segue una gran calca
Di gente . . . è già vicino . . .
Mentr'io vi parlo ei valca
L'ingresso . . .

FALSTAFF

Whom?

ALICE

Meg . . .

FALSTAFF

Good Grace! That old, repulsive
creature?

ALICE

Do not leave me, my John!

FALSTAFF

Insane with longing, I love your every
feature. Always . . .
(*He pursues her again, trying to embrace her.*)

ALICE (*defending herself*)

Please let me go!

FALSTAFF

(*putting his arms around her waist*)
Always!

QUICKLY

(*from offstage, screaming*)
Oh, Mistress Alice!

FALSTAFF

(*releasing Alice, confused*)
Who is that?

QUICKLY
(*entering, feigning excitement*)
Oh, Mistress Alice!

ALICE

What now?

QUICKLY
(*out of breath, stammering*)
Please forgive me! . . . 'Tis Mistress
Meg.
She wants to see you . . . trembling,
staggering, and rattled.

FALSTAFF

Speak of the Devil!

QUICKLY

She's at the door. I could not bar her
entry.

FALSTAFF

Where can I hide?

ALICE

The screen here will conceal you.
(*Falstaff hides behind the screen. As
soon as he is out of sight, Quickly
motions Meg to enter. Meg enters,
pretending to be highly agitated.
Quickly turns to leave again.*)

MEG

Oh, dear me! What an uproar! What
turmoil! What commotion! Away
from here and quickly! Hurry!

ALICE

My Goodness gracious! What
happened?

MEG

Your husband's voice shakes every roof-
top and girder, Howling. . . .

ALICE

(*under her breath, to Meg*)
Can you speak louder?

MEG

. . . that he is bent on murder.
(*almost bursting out with laughter*)

ALICE

(*under her breath*)
Contain yourself!

MEG

He is on his way, insane and frantic
with rage,
And even curses women in bitter fury.

ALICE

My Goodness gracious!

MEG

Sure that you're concealing a lover
He promises to skin him alive.

QUICKLY

(*returning in great agitation, screaming
even louder than before.*)
May Heaven help us! 'Tis Master
Ford!
Go, hide yourself! He'll tear us all
asunder.
Deafening, roaring, shattering,
He's rolling in like thunder,
Violent and delirious.

ALICE

(*somewhat alarmed, under her breath
to Quickly*)
In jest or are you serious?

QUICKLY

I'm serious. In wild vexation,
A crowd of people near him,
As red as a carnation,
He's running . . . I seem to hear him!
Oh think of your salvation . . .
    I pray you . . .

FORD
(*di dentro urlando*)
Malandrino!!!

FALSTAFF
(*Sgomentatissimo avrà già fatto un passo per fuggire dal paravento, ma udendo la voce dell'uomo torna a rimpiattarsi.*)
Il diavolo cavalca sull'arco di un violino!!
(*Alice, con una mossa rapidissima, lo chiude nei paravento, in modo che non è più veduto.*
Alice, Meg, Quickly, Mr. Ford, poi subito il Dr. Cajus, poi Fenton, poi Bardolfo e Pistola, poi Nannetta, Falstaff sempre nascosto nel paravento.)

FORD
(*dal fondo gridando rivolto a chi lo segue.*)
Chiudete le porte! Sbarrate le scale! Seguitemi a caccia! Scoviamo il cignale!
(*Entrano correndo il Dr. Cajus e Fenton.*)
Correte sull'orme, sull'usta.
(*a Fenton*)
Tu fruga negli anditi.

BARDOLFO, PISTOLA
(*Irrompono nella sala gridando, mentre Fenton corre a sinistra.*)
A caccia!

FORD
(*a Bardolfo e Pistola, indicando la camera a destra*)
Sventate la fuga! Cercate là dentro!
(*a Bardolfo e Pistola si precipitano nella camera coi bastoni levati.*)

ALICE
(*affrontando Ford*)
Sei tu dissennato? Che fai?

FORD
(*Vede il cesto.*)
Chi c'è dentro quel cesto?

ALICE
Il bucato.

FORD
(*ad Alice*)
Mi lavi!! rea moglie!
(*consegnando un mazzo di chiavi al Dr. Cajus, che escirà correndo dall' uscio di sinistra*)
Tu, piglia le chiavi,
Rovista le casse!
(*ad Alice*)
Ben tu mi lavi!
(*Dà un calcio alla cesta.*)
Al diavolo i cenci!
(*gridando verso il fondo*)

Sprangatemi l'uscio del parco!
(*Estrae furiosamente la biancheria dalla cesta, frugando e cercando dentro, e disseminando i panni sul pavimento.*)

Camicie . . . gonnelle . . . - Or ti sguscio, briccon! - Stronfinacci! Via! Via! cuffie rotte! - Ti sguscio. - Lenzuola . . .berretti da notte . . . - Non c'è . . .
(*Rovescia la cesta.*)

ALICE, MEG, QUICKLY
(*guardando i panni sparsi*)
Che uragano!!

FORD
(*correndo e gridando, esce dalla porta a sinistra*)
Cerchiam sotto il letto, nel forno, nel Bagno, sul tetto, in cantina . . .

ALICE
È farnetico!

QUICKLY
Cogliam tempo.

ALICE
Troviamo modo com'egli esca.

MEG
Nel panier.

ALICE
No, là dentro non c'entra, è troppo grosso.

FALSTAFF
(*Sbalordito, ode le parole d'Alice, sbuca e corre alla cesta.*)
Vediam; sì, c'entro, c'entro.

ALICE
Corro a chiamare i servi.   (*Esce.*)

MEG
(*a Falstaff, fingendo sorpresa*)
Sir John! Voi qui? Voi?

FALSTAFF
(*entrando nella cesta*)
T'amo! Amo te sola . . . salvami! salvami!

FORD

(*screaming from offstage*)

I will spear him!

FALSTAFF

(*He already has set out to flee but stays when hearing Ford's voice. Alice folds the screen around him to conceal him completely.*)

Those fiddles spell damnation and give me cause to fear him!

FORD

(*from upstage, shouting to those who follow him*)

Now block all the doorways and watch in the alley!
We'll see the seducer in chains on a galley!

(*After Ford enter Dr. Cajus and Fenton, shortly afterwards Bardolph and Pistol.*)

(*to Cajus*)

You follow his scent till you find him!

(*to Fenton*)

Explore all the passages!

BARDOLPH, PISTOL

To action!

FORD

(*to Bardolph and Pistol, pointing to the right*)

Cut off his escape and examine the pantry!

ALICE

(*somewhat haughtily, to Ford*)

You seem to be crazy . . . but why?

FORD

(*noticing the basket*)

Well, well . . . what's in the basket?

ALICE

Dirty linen.

FORD (*to Alice*)

Yes, dirty, quite dirty!

(*to Cajus, handing him a bunch of keys*)

Go, here are the keys to the cupboards and caskets.

(*to Alice*)

Angel of virtue!!!

(*kicking the basket*)

To hell with these tatters!

(*shouting towards the rear*)

Go on, reconnoiter the garden!

(*starts pulling the wash out of the basket, strewing it all over the floor*)

The drawers . . . and blouses . . . now I'll catch you, you lout!
. . . dirty napkins, out! Out!
Here some stockings! I'll catch you . . . and bedsheets . . .
. . . some silly old nightcaps . . . not yet!

(*searching furiously*)

ALICE, MEG, QUICKLY

(*looking at the scattered wash*)

Howling tempest!

FORD

(*running to and fro, yelling to all and sundry*)

Go, search in the attic, the cistern, the arbor,
The kitchen, the bedroom and the cellar!

(*off to the left*)

ALICE

He's a lunatic!

QUICKLY

Let us hurry!

ALICE

How can our portly friend escape him?

MEG

In the basket!

ALICE

No, it never will hold him. He's far too bulky.

FALSTAFF

(*coming out from behind the screen*)

Let's see!

(*squeezing himself into the basket*)

Ah . . . it is . . . easy . . .

ALICE

I'll go to call the servants.

(*off to the rear*)

MEG

(*to Falstaff, feigning surprise*)

Sir John, you here . . . you?

FALSTAFF

(*still fighting the basket*)

Angel! Only beloved! Help me now! Rescue me!

QUICKLY

(*a Falstaff, raccattando i panni*)

Svelto!

MEG

Lesto!

FALSTAFF

(*accovacciandosi con grande sforzo nella cesta*)

Ahi! . . . Ahi! . . . Ci sto . . .
Copritemi . . .

QUICKLY

Presto! colmiamo il cesto.

(*Fra tutte due con gran fretta ricacciano la biancheria nel cesto.*

Meg e Quickly attendono a nascondere Falstaff sotto la biancheria, mentre Nannetta e Fenton entrano da sinistra.)

NANNETTA

(*sottovoce, con cautela a Fenton*)

Vien qua.

FENTON

Che chiasso!

NANNETTA

Quanti schiamazzi! Segui il mio passo.

FENTON

Casa di pazzi!

NANNETTA

Qui ognun delira
Con vario error.
Son pazzi d'ira . . .

FENTON

E noi d'amor.

NANNETTA

(*Lo prende per mano, lo conduce dietro il paravento e vi si nascondono.*)

Seguimi. Adagio.

FENTON

Nessun m'ha scorto.

NANNETTA

Tocchiamo il porto.

FENTON

Siamo a nostr'agio.

NANNETTA

Sta zitto e attento.

FENTON (*abbracciandola*)

Vien sul mio petto!

NANNETTA

Il paravento . . .

NANNETTA, FENTON

Sia benedetto!

(*Nannetta e Fenton nascosti nel paravento. Mr. Ford ed il Dr. Cajus da sinistra, Bardolfo e Pistola da destra con Gente del vicinato. Quickly e Meg accanto alla cesta dove c'è Falstaff nascosto. Poi ritornerà Alice dal fondo.*)

DR. CAJUS

(*urlando di dentro*)

Al ladro!

FORD (*come sopra*)

Al pagliardo!

DR. CAJUS

(*Entra, traversando di corsa la sala.*)

Squartatelo!

FORD (*come sopra*)

Al ladro! C'è?

(*incontrando Bardolfo e Pistola che corrono da destra*)

PISTOLA

No.

FORD (*a Bardolfo*)

C'è?

BARDOLFO

Non c'è, no.

FORD

(*correndo, cercando e frugando nella cassapanca*)

Vada a soqquadro la casa.

DR. CAJUS

(*dopo aver guardato nel camino*)

Non trovo nessuno.

(*Bardolfo e Pistola escono da sinistra.*)

FORD

Eppur giuro che l'uomo è qua dentro.
Ne sono sicuro! Sicuro! Sicuro!

DR. CAJUS

Sir John! Sarò gaio
Quel dì ch'io ti veda dar calci a rovaio!

FORD

(*slanciandosi contro l'armadio e facendo sforzi per aprirlo*)

Vien fuora, furfante! O bombardo le mura!

DR. CAJUS

(*Tenta aprire l'armadio colle chiavi.*)

T'arrendi!

QUICKLY

(*to Falstaff, collecting the pieces of wash*)

Hurry!

MEG

Head down!

FALSTAFF

(*making a supreme effort to squeeze fully into the basket*)

Ah, ouch! I'm in. Now cover me!

QUICKLY

Grumble before you tumble!

(*The women cover him with wash.*)

(*Ann and Fenton enter from the left, speaking softly and cautiously.*)

ANN

Come here!

FENTON

I worry!

ANN

Don't be so lazy! Come, let us hurry!

FENTON

All this is crazy!

ANN

See how they're fuming, jostle and shove,
As mad with fury . . .

FENTON

. . . as we with love!

ANN

(*taking him by the hand to pull him behind the screen*)

Follow me, but lightly!

FENTON

I'm here beside you.

ANN

The screen will hide you . . .

FENTON

. . . shielding us tightly.

ANN

We're safe from detection.

FENTON

(*drawing her close*)

Let me caress you!

ANN

Welcome protection,

BOTH

. . . Fondly we bless you!

(*Ann and Fenton are hiding behind the screen. Enter Ford and Cajus from the left, Bardolph and Pistol from the right, together with a group of neighbors. Quickly and Meg stay near the basket where Falstaff is hidden. Later Alice returns from the rear.*)

DR. CAJUS

(*yelling from the outside*)

Behead him! (*enters*)

FORD (*still outside*)

To the gallows! (*enters*)

DR. CAJUS

. . . and quarter him!

FORD

The scoundrel! There?

(*On their way in, Ford and Cajus collide with Pistol and Bardolph.*)

PISTOL

No.

FORD (*to Bardolph*)

There?

BARDOLPH

Not here! No.

FORD

(*running about, searching the chest*)

I vow to Satan I'll find him!

DR. CAJUS

(*searching in the fire-place and looking up the chimney*)

Where is he, I wonder.

(*Pistol and Bardolph exit to the left.*)

FORD

I swear he still is here in the house.
Yes, I know it for certain, I know it for certain.

DR. CAJUS

Sir John, I'll be dying with laughter
The day you will hang from the rafter.

FORD

(*trying to break open the cupboard*)

Come out here, you ronyon, or I'll tear you to tatters!

DR. CAJUS

(*looking for a key to the cupboard*)

Surrender!

FORD
Vien fuora! Codardo! Sugliardo!

BARDOLFO, PISTOLA
(dalla porta di sinistra, di corsa)
Nessuno!

FORD
(a Bardolfo e Pistola, mentre continua
a sforzare l'arma dio col Dr. Cajus)
Cercatelo ancora! T'arrendi!
Scanfardo!
(Bardolfo e Pistola ritornano subito
d'onde erano venuti.
Riesce finalmente ad aprire l'armadio.)
Non c'è!!

DR. CAJUS
(aprendo a sua volta la cassapanca)
Vieni furora! Non c'è!
(Gira per la sala sempre cercando e
frugando.)
Pappalardo! Beòn! Bada a te!

FORD
(come un ossesso aprendo il cassetto
del tavolino)
Scagnardo! Falsardo! Briccon!!
(Nannetta e Fenton, sempre dietro il
paravento, si saran fatte moine dur-
ante il frastuono.)

NANNETTA E FENTON
(Si danno un baccio sonoro nel pasto
del verso marcato dall'asterisco)
(*)!
(In questo punto è cessato il baccano e
tutti sentono il susurro del bacio.)

(nel paravento)

NANNETTA (a Fenton)

Mentre quei vecchi
Corron la giostra,
Noi di sottecchi
Corriam la nostra.
L'amor non ode
Tuon nè bufere,
Vola alle sfere
Beate e gode.

FENTON (a Nannetta)

Bella! ridente!
Oh! come pieghi
Verso i miei prieghi
Donnescamente!
Come ti vidi
M'innamorai
E tu sorridi
Perche io sai.

FORD
(sottovoce, guardando il paravento)
C'è.

DR. CAJUS (come sopra)
C'è.

FORD
(avviandosi pian piano e cautamente
al paravento)
Se t'agguanto!

DR. CAJUS (come sopra)
Se ti piglio!

FORD
Se t'acciuffo!

DR. CAJUS
Se t'acceffo!

FORD
Ti sconquasso!

DR. CAJUS
T'arronciglio come un can!

FORD
Ti rompo il ceffo!

DR. CAJUS
Guai a te!

FORD
Prega il tuo santo!
Guai se alfin con te m'azzuffo!
Se ti piglio!

DR. CAJUS
Se t'agguanto!

FORD
Se t'acceffo!

DR. CAJUS
Se t'acciuffo!

(intorno alla cesta)

QUICKLY
(accanto alla cesta, a Meg)

Facciamo le viste
D'attendere ai panni;
Pur ch'ei non c'inganni
Con mosse impreviste.
Finor non s'accorse
Di nulla; egli può
Sorprenderci forse,
Confonderci no.

MEG
(accanto alla cesta, a Quickly)

Facciamogli siepe
Fra tanto scompiglio.
Ne' giuochi il periglio
È un grano di pepe.
Il rischio è un diletto
Che accresce l'ardor,
Che stimola in petto
Gli spiriti e il cor.

FORD

Come out here, you traitor! You coward!

BARDOLPH, PISTOL

(*re-entering from the left*)

There's no one!

FORD

(*still busy, with Dr. Cajus, trying to open the cupboard while Bardolph and Pistol re-exit to where they came from*)

You filthy rapscallion! Surrender, you demon!

(*finally opening the cupboard*)

Not here?

DR. CAJUS

(*opening the chest*)

Surrender! Not here?

(*runs through the room, searching*)

You debaucher, you'll wish you were dead!

FORD

(*opening the drawer of the little table*)

You Satan, you lecher, you villain, you lout . . . come out!

(*During all this, Ann and Fenton have paid no heed to the turmoil around them. Their caresses come to a head in a resounding kiss which immediately stops all activity. Everyone has heard the sound of the kiss.*)

FORD

(*whispering, his eyes on the screen*)

There!

DR. CAJUS

There!

(*Everyone's attention now centers on the screen.*)

FORD

(*cautiously approaching the screen*)

When I catch you . . .

DR. CAJUS (*imitating Ford*)

When I snatch you . . .

FORD

When I grab you . . .

DR. CAJUS

When I nab you . . .

FORD

I will thrash you, . . .

DR. CAJUS

I will break your every bone . . .

FORD

. . . beat up and smash you.

DR. CAJUS

. . . with a stone!

FORD

No one can save you.

(*behind the screen*)

ANN (*to Fenton*)

They yell and chatter
Hunting their quarry.
What does it matter,
We shall not worry.
Thunder and lightning
To us are not fright'ning
Onward we fly, like doves
On golden wings of love.

FENTON (*to Ann*)

So sweet and tender
I feel you near me,
Forever cheer me
Your radiant splendor
I stood before you,
Under your spell . . .
How I adore you . . .
You know it well!

(*near the basket*)

QUICKLY (*to Meg*)

Our friend in the basket,
You cannot deny it,
Unless he is quiet
Turns basket to casket.
He wants to disarm us
But progress is slow.
He still may alarm us,
But harm us, oh no!

MEG (*to Quickly*)

Our cunning devices
At first lead to shambles,
Providing our gambles
With savor and spices.
We're taking our chances
As never before,
But danger enhances
Our fun even more.

FALSTAFF
(*sbucando colla faccia*)
Affogo!

QUICKLY
(*ricacciandolo giù*)
Sta sotto.

BARDOLFO
(*rientrando da sinistra*)
Non si trova.

PISTOLA
(*rientrando con alcuni del vicinato*)
Non si coglie.

FORD
(*a Bardolfo, Pistola e loro compagni*)
Psss . . . Qua tutti.
(*indicando il paravento*)
L'ho trovato.
Là c'è Falstaff con mia moglie.

BARDOLFO
Sozzo can vituperato!

FORD
Zitto!

PISTOLA, DR. CAJUS
Zitto!!

FORD (*a Bardolfo*)
Urlerai dopo.
Là s'è udito il suon d'un bacio.

BARDOLFO
Noi dobbiam pigliare il topo
Mentre sta rodendo il cacio.

FORD
Ragioniam. Colpo non vibro
Senza un piano di battaglia.

NANNETTA
Lo spiritello d'amor, volteggia.

FENTON
Già un sogno bello d'Imene albeggia.

NANNETTA
Tutto delira,
Sospiro e riso.
Sorride il viso
E il cor sospira.
Come in sua zolla
Si schiude un fior,
Svolve il mio cor.
La sua corolla

FORD
Senti, accosta un po' l'orecchio!
Che patetici lamenti!!
Su quel nido d'usignuoli
Scoppierà fra poco il tuon.

BARDOLFO
È la voce della donna
Che risponde al cavalier.

FALSTAFF
(*intorno alla cesta*)
Affogo!

MEG
Or questi s'insorge.

QUICKLY
(*abbassandosi e parlando a Falstaff sulla cesta*)
Se l'altro ti scorge
Sei morto.

DR. CAJUS
Un uom di quel calibro
Con un soffio ci sbaraglia.

FORD
La mia tattica maestra
Le sue mosse pria registra.
(*a Pistola e a due compagni*)
Voi sarete l'ala destra,
(*a Bardolfo e al Dr. Cajus*)
Noi sarem l'ala sinistra.
(*agli altri compagni*)
E costor con pie' gagliardo
Sfonderanno il baluardo.

TUTTI GLI ALTRI
Bravo, bravo Generale.

DR. CAJUS
Aspettiamo un tuo segnale.

GLI ALTI
Bravo.

MEG
Il ribaldo vorrebbe un ventaglio

FALSTAFF
Un breve spiraglio non chiedo di più.

QUICKLY
Ti metto il bavaglio se parli. Giù!

FENTON
Fra quelle ciglia
Vedo due fari
A meraviglia
Sereni e chiari.
Bocca mia dolce
Pupilla d'or.
Voce che molce
Com'arpa il cor.

DR. CAJUS
Sento, sento sento, intendo,
E vedo chiaro.
Delle femmine,
Delle femmine gl'inganni.

PISTOLA
Ma fra poco il lieto gioco
Egli canta, ma fra poco
Muterà la sua canzon.

FALSTAFF
(*poking his head out of the basket*)
I'm choking.
QUICKLY
(*pushing him down*)
Lie low and keep quiet!

BARDOLPH
(*entering from the left*)
It is useless.
PISTOL
(*returning with several neighbors*)
We can't find him!

FORD
(*to Bardolph, Pistol, and the others*)
Pssst . . . be quiet!
(*pointing to the screen*)
I have found him.
With my wife he's there in hiding.

BARDOLPH
What a scandal, what an outrage!

FORD
Silence!
PISTOL, DR. CAJUS
Silence!
FORD (*to Bardolph*)
You hold your thunder!
We have heard the sound of kisses.

BARDOLPH
In this case of sinful blisses
Slay the man and spare the missus!

FORD
Not so fast! Now pay attention!
We shall draw a plan of battle.

ANN
The stars above web a veil around us.

FENTON
The God of Love has forever bound us.

ANN
Trying to flee you,
Sighing, delirious,
My heart mysterious
Cries out to see you.
Sweet is the torment of love!
Yes, I shall love you forever.

FORD
Bend an ear and you can hear them!
Hear their billing and their cooing!
From this hotbed of misdoing
I'll dispatch him to the moon.

BARDOLPH
I am certain 'tis the woman
Answering her lover's call.

FALSTAFF (*in the basket*)
I'm smoking.
MEG
(*pushing him down*)
'Tis good for your diet.

QUICKLY
(*bending down and addressing Falstaff in the basket*)
You're causing a riot, be quiet!

DR. CAJUS
A man of vast dimension,
He may slaughter us like cattle.

FORD
I'm a master at deception,
Let me tell you my conception:
(*to Pistol and two neighbors*)
While the right wing will dislodge him
(*to Bardolph and Dr. Cajus*)
On the left you'll draw and dodge him.
(*to everyone else*)
Then the center under cover
Will exterminate our lover.

THE OTHERS
What a fine display of cunning!

DR. CAJUS
Tell us when and we'll be running.

THE OTHER MEN
Truly stunning!
MEG
How much more can we do for his comfort?
FALSTAFF
Just one single breath or in clothes I will drown!
QUICKLY
You're courting your death, so be silent!
Go down!

FENTON
Your eyes shall meet me,
Radiant, beguiling,
Like starlets smiling
Come down to greet me.
Tell me you love me!
I love you always.

DR. CAJUS
Yes, I hear them, I perceive it
But can't believe it.
Can it really be . . .
Can a woman be so bold?

PISTOL
If he knew that we are near him!
In a moment I shall spear him:
I should say 'tis none to soon.

CORO

S'egli cade più non scappa,
Nessun più lo può salvar.
Nel tuo diavolo t'incappa;
Che tu possa stramazzar!

MEG

Parliam sottovoce
Guardando il Messer
Che brontola e cuoce
Nel nostro panier.

QUICKLY

Costui s'è infardato
Di tanta viltà,
Che darlo al bucato
È averne pietà.

FORD

Zitto! A noi! Quest'è il momento.
Zitto! Attenti! Attenti a me.

FALSTAFF

Ouff . . . Cesto molesto!

ALICE

Silenzio!

FALSTAFF

Protesto!

MEG, QUICKLY

Che bestia restìa!

FALSTAFF

Portatemi via!

DR. CAJUS

Dà il segnal.

MEG, QUICKLY

È matto furibondo

FALSTAFF

Aiuto! aiuto! aiuto!

FORD

Uno . . . Due . . . Tre . . .
(*Rovesciando il paravento*)

DR. CAJUS

Non è lui!!

(*Nannetta e Fenton, nel rovesciando del paravento, rimangono scoperti e confusi*).

TUTTI

Sbalordimento!

FORD

(*a Nannetta con furia*)
Ancor nuove rivolte!
(*a Fenton*)
Tu va pe' fatti tuoi!
L'ho detto mille volte: Costei non fa
per voi.
(*Nannetta sbigottita fugge e Fenton esce dal fondo.*)

BARDOLFO

(*correndo verso il fondo*)
È là! Ferma!

FORD

Dove?

PISTOLA

Là! sulle scale.

FORD

Squartatelo!

PISTOLA, BARDOLFO, DR. CAJUS ED I
COMPAGNI

A caccia!

QUICKLY

Che caccia infernale!
(*Tutti gli uomini salgono a corsa la scala del fondo.*)

ALICE (*scampanellando*)

Ned! Will! Tom! Isäac! Su! Presto!
Presto!
(*Nannetta rientra con quattro servi e un paggetto.*)
Rovesciate quel cesto
Dalla finestra nell'acqua del fosso . . .
Là! presso alle giuncaie
Davanti al crocchio delle lavandaie.

NANNETTA, MEG E QUICKLY

Sì, sì, sì, sì!

CHORUS OF NEIGHBORS

Sinful love may bring you glory
While the sinning's going well:
'Twill be quite another story
When you pay for it in Hell.

MEG

We better defy him
And better beware.
'Tis better to fry him
Than render him rare.

QUICKLY

'Tis really a quandary:
So black is our swain,
That even a laundry
Won't clean him again.

FORD

Silence! Stand by! This is our moment.
Silence! Attention! And follow me!

FALSTAFF

(gasping for air)

Oh, oh, hear me crying!

ALICE

(having returned to the basket)

Be quiet!

FALSTAFF (emerging again)
I'm dying!

MEG, QUICKLY
Why, how can you dare it?

FALSTAFF (in agony)
Ah, I cannot bear it!

DR. CAJUS (to Ford)
Tell us when!

MEG, QUICKLY
He must have lost his senses.

FALSTAFF

Oh, help me! Oh, help me! Oh, help
me!

(The women push him down and sit on
the basket.)

FORD

One . . . two . . . three ! ! ! ! ! ! !

(On the count of "Three" the men
open the screen, revealing Ann and
Fenton in tender embrace. Utmost
consternation is on everyone's face.)

DR. CAJUS
Where is he?

ALL
The search has ended!

FORD

(to Ann, furiously)

A fine way to behold you!

(to Fenton)

From now on you'll obey.
How often have I told you;
Keep off my daughter's way!

(Ann flees disconsolately. Fenton leaves
through the rear.)

BARDOLPH

(running to the rear)

He's there! Stop him!

FORD

Where?

PISTOL

There, on the staircase!

FORD

Take hold of him!

CAJUS, BARDOLPH, PISTOL, NEIGHBORS
We'll catch him.

(All run off towards the rear.)

QUICKLY
I wish them good hunting!

ALICE

(calling to the rear)

Ned! Will! Tom! And Jack!

(Ann returns with four servants and a
page.)

Come! Come here quickly!
Go and empty this basket out of the
window and into the river, there,
where you see the women about to
launder all the dirty linen!

ANN, MEG, QUICKLY
Yes, yes, yes, yes!

NANNETTA

(*ai servi, che s'affaticano a sollevare la cesta*)

C'è dentro un pezzo grosso.

ALICE

(*al paggetto, che poi esce dalla scala nel fondo*)

Tu chiama mio marito;

(*a Meg, mentre Nannetta e Quickly stanno a guardare i servi che avranno sollevata la cesta*)

Gli narreremo il nostro caso pazzo.
Solo al vedere il Cavalier nel guazzo.
D'ogni gelosa ubbìa sarà guarito.

QUICKLY (*ai servi*)

Pesa!

ALICE, MEG

(*ai servi, che sono già vicini alla finestra*)

Coraggio!

NANNETTA

Il fondo ha fatta crac!

MEG, QUICKLY, NANNETTA

Su!

ALICE

Trionfo! Che tonfo!

(*La cesta, Falstaff e la biancheria capitombolano giù dalla finestra.*)

NANNETTA, MEG

Che tonfo!

(*Gran grido e risata di donne dall' estrano: immensa risata di Alice, Nannetta, Meg e Quickly. Ford e gli altri uomini rientrano. Alice vedendo Ford lo piglia per un braccio e lo conduce rapidamente alla finestra.*)

TUTTI

Patatrac!

ATTO TERZO

PARTE PRIMA

Un piazzale.

A destra l'esterno dell'Osteria della Giarrettiera coll'insegna e il motto: "Honny soit qui mal y pense." Una panca di fianco al portone. È l'ora del tramonto.

FALSTAFF

(*seduto sulla panca, meditando. Poi si scuote, dà un gran pugno sulla panca e rivolto verso l'interno dell'osteria chiama l'Oste.*)

Ehi! Taverniere!

(*Ritorna meditabondo.*)

Mondo ladro - Mondo rubaldo. Reo mondo!

(*Entra l'Oste.*)

Taverniere: un bicchier di vin caldo.

(*l'Oste riceve l'ordine e rientra.*)

Io, dunque, avrò vissuto tanti anni, audace e destro
Cavaliere, per essere portato in un canestro
E gittato al canale coi pannilini biechi,
Come si fa coi gatti e i catellini ciechi.
Che se non galleggiava per me quest'epa tronfia
Certo affogavo. Brutta morte. L'acqua mi gonfia.
Mondo reo. Non c'è più virtù. Tutto declina.
Va, vecchio John, va, va per la tua via; cammina
Finchè tu muoia. Allor scomparirà la vera
Virilità dal mondo.
Che giornataccia nera!
M'aiuti il ciel! Impinguo troppo. Ho dei peli grigi.

(*Ritorna l'Oste portando su d'un vassoio un gran bicchiere di vino caldo. Mette il bicchiere sulla panca e rientra all'osteria.*)

Versiamo un po' di vino nell'acqua del Tamigi.

(*Beve sorseggiando ed assaporando. Si sbottona il panciotto, si sdraia, ribeve a sorsate, rainimandosi poco a poco.*)

Buono. Ber del vin dolce e sbottonarsi al sole,
Dolce cosa! Il buon vino sperde le tetre fole
Dello sconforto, accende l'occhio e il pensier, dal labbro
Sale al cervel e quivi risveglia il picciol fabbro
Dei trilli; un negro grillo che vibra entro l'uom brillo
Trilla ogni fibra in cor, l'allegro etere al trillo
Guizza e il giocondo globo squilibra una demenza
Trillante! E il trillo invade il mondo!!! . . .

ANN

(*to the servants trying to lift the basket*)
It may be somewhat heavy.

ALICE

(*to the page who obeys her request*)
You go and call my master . . .

(*to Meg, while Ann and Quickly watch
the servants lifting the basket*)

. . . so he may witness old Sir John's
disaster.
Seeing his rival in this sad condition
Should cool his own suspicion
That much faster.

QUICKLY

(*to the servants*)

Try it!

ALICE, MEG

(*to the servants approaching the
window*)

Come on now!

ANN

The bottom will fall out. Up!

ALICE

Upend it! That's splendid!
(*The contents of the basket tumble out
the window.*)

ANN, MEG

That's splendid!
(*A loud scream and gales of laughter
of the women outside. At that moment Ford and the other men return
to the room.*)

ALL

What a splash!—
(*Alice takes her husband's arm and
quickly leads him to the window.
Great hilarity all around.*)

ACT THREE

PART ONE

An open square.

(*To the right the Garter Inn with the
sign inscribed HONY SOIT QUI
MAL Y PENSE. Next to the entrance a bench of stone. It is near
sunset. Falstaff is seated on the
bench, deep in thought. Suddenly he
shakes himself violently, pounds the
bench with his fist and calls for the
innkeeper.*)

FALSTAFF

Ho! Is there no one?

(*sinks back into meditation*)

Nasty world! Villanous world! Vile
world!

(*The innkeeper appears.*)

Bring some wine here! Serve it hot to
revive me!

(*the innkeeper exits.*)

John Falstaff who led a life of adventure, a noble knight, a gallant fighter,
at last has had to cower in a basket
to be dumped into a ditch with a load
of dirty linen as if he were a cat or
some repulsive mongrel!
Unless my mighty paunch like a cork
had kept me floating I should have
perished, filled with water, swelling
and bloating.
Rotten world!
All has run to seed. Virtue is crumbling.
Go, gallant John, go, go onward to
glory!
Go on till you end your journey!
With you once and for all will die the
enchanted flow'r of manhood.
What an infernal nightmare! My gracious Lord!
I grow too portly, my hair is turning
grey . . .

(*The innkeeper brings a large goblet of
hot wine and deposits it on the bench,
then exits.*)

I trust this bracing potion
will warm the icy ocean!

(*He drinks slowly, savoring every sip.
Then he unbuttons his vest, stretches
comfortably, drinks again. His mood
is changing for the better.*)

Splendid! To drink good wine is to enjoy the sunshine, warm and tender.
All at once, good wine will dispel the
clouds of sorrow and worry, revive
the heart and the eye.
Your mind will flutter and fly while
millions of bells will ring in joyous
carillon . . .
And slyly winking a goblin keeps you
drinking.
Trilling its siren-song, the wine thrills
us all, cruel or tender. And a world
contented, delirious in its folly, demented, shall willingly surrender!

QUICKLY

(*inchinandosi e interrompendo Falstaff*)

Reverenza. La bella Alice . . .

FALSTAFF

(*alzandosi e scattando*)

Al diavolo te con Alice bella!
Ne ho piene le bisaccie! Ne ho piene le budella!

QUICKLY

Voi siete errato . . .

FALSTAFF

Un canchero!! Sento ancor le cornate
Di quell'irco geloso! Ho ancor l'ossa arrembate
D'esser rimasto curvo, come una buona lama
Di Bilbào, nello spazio d'un panierin di dama!
Con quel tufo! E quel caldo! Un uom della mia tempra,
Che in uno stillicidio continuo si distempra!
Poi, quando fui ben cotto, rovente, incandescente,
M'han tuffato nell'acqua. Canaglie!!!

(*Alice, Meg, Nannetta, Mr. Ford, Dr. Cajus, Fenton sbucano dietro una casa, or l'uno or l'altro spiando, non visti da Falstaff e poi si nascondono, poi tornano a spiare.*)

QUICKLY

Essa è innocente.
Prendete abbaglio.

FALSTAFF

Vattene!!

QUICKLY (*infervorata*)

La colpa è di quei fanti
Malaugurati! Alice piange, urla, invoca i santi.
Povera donna! V'ama. Leggete.

(*Estrae di tasca una lettera. Falstaff la prende e si mette a leggere.*)

ALICE

(*nel fondo sottovoce agli altri, spiando*)

Legge.

FORD (*sottovoce*)

Legge.

NANNETTA

Vedrai che ci ricasca.

ALICE

L'uom non si corregge.

MEG

(*ad Alice, vedendo un gesto nascosto di Mrs. Quickly*)

Nasconditi.

DR. CAJUS

Rilegge.

FORD

Rilegge. L'esca inghiotte.

FALSTAFF

(*rileggendo ad alta voce e con molta attenzione*)

T'aspetterò nel parco Real, a mezzanotte
Tu verrai travestito da Cacciatore nero
Alla quercia di Herne.

QUICKLY

Amor ama il mistero.
Per rivedervi Alice, si val d'una leggenda
Popolar. Quella quercia è un luogo da tregenda.
Il Cacciatore nero s'è impeso ad un suo ramo.
V'ha chi crede vederlo ricomparir . . .

FALSTAFF

(*Rabbonito prende per un braccio Mrs. Quickly e s'avvia per entrare con essa nell'osteria.*)

Entriamo. Là si discorre meglio.
Narrami la tua frasca.

QUICKLY

(*Incominciando il racconto della leggenda con mistero, entra nell'osteria con Falstaff.*)

Quando il rintocco della mezzanotte . . .

FORD

(*dal fondo*)

Ci casca.

QUICKLY

(interrupting Falstaff's happy musings)

I am honored! Fair Mistress Alice. . . .

FALSTAFF (rising violently)

Go, take her to Hell and remain there forever!
The Devil will adore her . . . for me she is too clever.

QUICKLY

You are mistaken . . .

FALSTAFF

I know her now, and my ears are still aching
From the screams of her husband,
My broken bones still shaking,
Tossed in a tiny basket, my body bent as if it were
A blade of Spanish steel, hilt to point and head to heel!
Madmen shrieking! Linen reeking!
I, melting like a candle
In heat that even Satan would find too hot to handle!
Then, while I'd burn like tinder
And slowly would turn to cinder,
In the end they would drown me!
Those rascals!

(Alice, Meg, Ann, Ford, Cajus, and Fenton are seen hiding behind a building to the left. They listen intently, emerging in turn from their hiding-place.)

QUICKLY

But she is blameless, completely blameless!
She could do nothing . . .

FALSTAFF

Out with you!

QUICKLY (feverishly)

The fault lay with those duffers whom she despises!
She is in torment, crying
Ah, how she suffers! Unhappy woman!
See here, she loves you!

(She takes a letter from her pocket and hands it to Falstaff who starts reading it.)

ALICE

(in the background, whispering to the others)

Reading?

FORD

Reading!

ANN

His mien looks much more jolly.

ALICE

Man never sheds his folly.

MEG

(to Alice, alerted by a sign from Quickly)

Conceal yourself!

DR. CAJUS

He's reading.

FORD

He's nibbling and will swallow!

FALSTAFF

(re-reading the letter with great concentration)

"I shall await you on the stroke of midnight in the park.
You will come quite alone, in the guise of the Black Huntsman,
to the Oak of Herne."

QUICKLY

Mysterious but entrancing!
Longing to see you, fearing to fail,
Alice recalled an ancient tale.
You should know the Oak of Herne is haunted.
Clad all in black, a hunter was found hanging from its branches.
Weird and eerie, his ghost still is seen at night.

FALSTAFF

(taking Quickly by the arm and guiding her inside the Inn)

We'll enter. Let us converse in private!
Tell me that fearsome story!

QUICKLY

(starts to tell him the legend while entering the Inn)

Oft when the chimes of twelve o'clock have sounded,
Leaving the world in dark and silent gloom . . .

FORD

(from the background)

He's biting!

ALICE

(*avanzandosi con tutto il crocchio, com-
icamente e misteriosamente ripigliando il racconto di Mrs. Quickly*)

Quando il rintocco della mezzanotte
Cupo si sparge nel silente orror,
Sorgon gli spirti vagabondi a frotte
E vien nel parco il nero Cacciator.
Egli cammina lento, lento, lento,
Nel gran letargo della sepoltura.
S'avanza livido . . .

NANNETTA

Oh! che spavento

MEG

Già sento il brivido della paura!

ALICE

(*con voce naturale*)

Fandonie che ai bamboli
Raccontan le nonne
Con lunghi preamboli,
Per farli dormir.

ALICE, NANNETTA E MEG

Vendetta di donne
Non deve fallir.

ALICE

(*ripigliando il racconto*)

S'avanza livido e il passo converge
Al tronco ove esalò l'anima prava.
Sbucan le Fate. Sulla fronte egli erge
Due corna lunghe, lunghe, lunghe . . .

FORD

Brava.
Quelle corna saranno la mia gioia!

ALICE

Bada! tu pur ti meriti
Qualche castigatoia!

FORD

Perdona. Riconosco i miei demeriti.

ALICE

Ma guai se ancor ti coglie
Quella mania feroce
Di cercar dentro il guscio d'una noce
L'amante di tua moglie.
Ma il tempo stringe e vuol fantasia
lesta.

MEG

Affrettiam.

FENTON

Concertiam la mascherata.

ALICE

Nannetta!

NANNETTA

Eccola qua!

ALICE

(*a Nannetta*)

Sarai la Fata
Regina delle Fate, in bianca vesta
Chiusa in candido vel, cinta di rose.

NANNETTA

E canterò parole armonïose.

ALICE (*a Meg*)

Tu la verde sarai Ninfa silvana,
E la comare Quickly una befana.

NANNETTA

A meraviglia!
(*Scende la sera, la scena si oscura.*)

ALICE

Avrò con me dei putti
Che fingeran folletti
E spiritelli,
E diavoletti,
E pipistrelli,
E farfarelli.
Su Falstaff camuffato in manto e corni
Ci scaglieremo tutti.

NANNETTA, MEG, FENTON

Tutti! tutti!

ALICE

E lo tempesteremo
Finch'abbia confessata
La sua perversità.
Poi ci smaschereremo
E, pria che il ciel raggiorni,
La giuliva brigata
Se ne ritornerà.

MEG

Vien sera. Rincasiam.

ALICE

(*advancing in a huddle with the others, grotesquely and mysteriously imitating Quickley's narration*)

Oft when the chimes of twelve o'clock have sounded,
Leaving the world in dark and silent gloom,
Demons and ghosts will hold the Oak surrounded:
Back comes the Hunter arising from his tomb.
He is approaching slowly, slowly, slowly,
As though entranced and walking without waking,
His bones are clattering. . . .

ANN

Phantom unholy!

MEG

I feel my blood congeal . . . and I am shaking.

ALICE

(*resuming her natural tone of voice*)

A fancy-free, a fairytale,
For children to ponder,
To set them on their merry way
And lull them to sleep!

ALICE, ANN, MEG

Our hunter will wonder . . .
Our meeting we'll keep!

ALICE

(*resuming her narration*)

. . . his bones are clattering, he's reaching his station
Where long ago his life sadly had ended.
See, from his forehead, to his consternation,
Two horns keep growing, growing, growing . . .

FORD

Splendid!
May these horns bring me never-ending gladness!

ALICE

Now repent your inanity!
You and your jealous madness!

FORD

Forgive me . . . I am cured of my insanity!

ALICE

Beware lest your suspicion
Should once again discover
In the shell of a nut a secret lover
To mar your disposition!
But time is fleeting. Let's keep our wits about us!

MEG

You are right.

FENTON

. . . or the play will start without us!

ALICE

Now, Annie!

ANN

At your command!

ALICE

You'll play the part of the Queen of all the Fairies.
Your royal mantle shall be white
And your veil girdled by roses.

ANN

In tender song my heart sweetly reposes.

ALICE (*to Meg*)

You, dear Meg, clad in green,
Will be the Wood-Nymph,
And our dear Mistress Quickly shall be a sorceress.

ANN (*happily*)

Ah, this is priceless!

(*The evening falls. The scene turns darker and darker.*)

ALICE

A host of tiny tots will play
In most delightful roundelay
As ghostly pixies clad in grey
And devils who will haunt him.
Until we shall assault our lovelorn hunter
And mercilessly taunt him.

ANN, MEG, FENTON

Haunt him! Taunt him!

ALICE

Until the old offender
Is ready to surrender
And eat his humble pie . . .
Then, only then we'll free him
When quite contrite we see him.
Gaily laughing we'll flee him,
Bid him a fond good-bye!

MEG

Let's leave now, it is late.

ALICE

L'appuntamento è alla quercia di Herne.

FENTON

È inteso.

NANNETTA

A meraviglia! Oh! che allegro spavento!

ALICE, NANNETTA, FENTON

Addio.

MEG

Addio.

(*Alice, Nannetta, Fenton escono da sinistra, Meg da destra. Sul limitare a sinistra, Alice gridando a Meg che sara gia avviata ad andarsene da destra. In questo momento Mrs. Quickly esce dall'osteria e vedendo Ford e Dr. Cajus che parlano, sta ad origliare sulla soglia*).

ALICE (*a Meg*)

Provvedi le lanterne.

FORD (*al Dr. Cajus*)

Non dubitar, tu sposerai mia figlia.
Rammenti bene il suo travestimento?

DR. CAJUS

Cinta di rose, il vel bianco e la vesta.

ALICE

(*di dentro a sinistra gridando*)
Non ti scordar le maschere.

MEG

(*di dentro a destra gridando*)
No, certo.
Nè tu le raganelle!

FORD

(*continuando il discorso col Dr. Cajus*)
Io già disposi
La rete mia. Sul finir della festa
Verrete a me col volto ricoperto
Essa dal vel, tu da un mantel fratesco
E vi benedirò come due sposi.

DR. CAJUS

Siam d'accordo.

QUICKLY

(*sul limitare dell'osteria con gesto accorto verso i due che escono*)
Stai fresco!
(*Esce rapidamente da destra.*)
Nannetta! Ohè! Nannetta!
Nannetta! Ohè!

NANNETTA

(*di dentro a sinistra*)
Che c'è? Che c'è?

QUICKLY

Prepara la canzone della Fata.

NANNETTA

È preparata.

ALICE

(*di dentro a sinistra*)
Tu, non tardar.

QUICKLY

(*come sopra, più lontana*)
Chi prima arriva, aspetta.

PARTE SECONDA

Il Parco di Windsor.

Nel centro, la gran quercia di Herne. Nel fondo, l'argine d'un fosso. Fronde foltissime. Arbusti in fiore. È notte.

Si odono gli appelli lontani dei guardiaboschi. Il parco a poco a poco si rischiarerà coi raggi della luna.

Fenton, poi Nannetta vestita da Regina delle Fate. Alice, non mascherata portando sul braccio una cappa e in mano una maschera. Mrs. Quickly in gran cuffia e manto grigio da befana, un bastone e un brutto ceffo di maschera in mano. Poi Meg, vestita con dei veli verdi e mascherata.

FENTON

Dal labbro il canto estasïato vola
Pe' silenzi notturni e va lontano
E alfin ritrova un altro labbro umano
Che gli risponde colla sua parola.
Allor la nota che non è più sola
Vibra di gioia in un accordo arcano
E innamorando l'aer antelucano
Come altra voce al suo fonte rivola.
Quivi ripiglia suon, ma la sua cura
Tende sempre ad unir chi lo disuna.
Così baciai la disïata bocca!
«Bocca baciata non perde ventura ...»

ALICE

Are we agreed when we meet near the oak tree?

FENTON

At midnight!

ANN

Wish it were sooner! How divine and romantic!

ALICE, ANN, FENTON

Farewell now!

MEG

Till midnight!

(*Alice, Ann, and Fenton exeunt towards the left, Meg towards the right. Just before disappearing, Alice calls to Meg who is already out of sight. At the same time Quickly, leaving the Garter Inn, notices Ford and Cajus in confidential conversation and stops to eavesdrop on them.*)

ALICE (*to Meg*)

Do not forget the lanterns!

FORD (*to Cajus*)

You may be sure. Soon you will wed my daughter.

Do you remember the dress she will be wearing?

DR. CAJUS

Belt trimmed with roses, white her veil and her garment.

ALICE

(*calling from offstage left*)

You will provide the dominoes!

MEG

(*from offstage right*)

They're ready.

You bring the bones and rattles.

FORD

(*continuing his conversation with Cajus*)

My plan is laid, its success is certain:

Well disguised by a hood you will come to me as soon as all is over. Ann will be there, still hidden by her veil . . . and I shall bestow my blessing on the both of you.

DR. CAJUS

Fine suggestion!

QUICKLY

(*giving the two men a telling look, then disappearing rapidly to the right*)

No question!!!

(*from offstage right*)

Oh, Ann! Pst! My Annie, pst!

ANN (*from offstage*)

I'm here. What is it?

QUICKLY

You know the song of the Queen of the Fairies?

ANN

It never varies!

ALICE (*offstage*)

You will be late!

QUICKLY (*from faraway*)

The sooner there, the better!

PART TWO

Windsor Park.

In the center, the Oak of Herne. To the rear, indications of a gully. Thick foliage. Bushes in bloom. It is night.

In the distance the horn-calls of the foresters are heard. Gradually the forest is brightened by moonlight.

(*Fenton, later Ann disguised as Queen of the Fairies. Later Alice, not disguised, carrying a hood over one arm and a mask in her hand. Mrs. Quickly carrying the paraphernalia of her disguise as a witch, including a broomstick. Later Meg, garbed in green veils and wearing a mask.*)

FENTON

From burning lips my song of love enchanted,

Through the dark of the night so gently calling,

Shall fly beyond to where the stars are falling.

Until at last my ardent plea is granted.

Out of the long and lonely night around me

A tender song, a ray of light confound me.

Oh, magic song whose sounds always will bind me,

Oh, guide my loved one till at last she will find me!

Once you have brought her here, herald so tender,

You will soon have to die: You must surrender

Unto the silence of our burning kisses.

Just kiss me soon, and you always will do it!

NANNETTA
(lontana e avvicinandosi)
«Anzi rinnova come fa la luna.»

FENTON
*(slanciandosi verso la parte dove udì
la voce)*
Ma il canto muor nel bacio che lo
tocca.
*(Fenton vede Nannetta che entra e la
abbraccia.)*

ALICE
*(dividendo Fenton da Nannetta e ob-
bligandolo a vestire la cappa nera)*
Nossignore! Tu indossa questa cappa.

FENTON
*(aiutato da Alice e Nannetta ad in-
dossare la cappa)*
Che vuol dir ciò?

NANNETTA
Lasciati fare.

ALICE
Allaccia.

NANNETTA
(rimirando Fenton)
È un fraticel sguisciato dalla Trappa.

ALICE
*(frettolosa, aiutando Fenton ad allac-
ciare la maschera)*
Il tradimento che Ford ne minaccia
Tornar deve in suo scorno e in nostro
aiuto.

FENTON
Spiegatevi.

ALICE
Ubbidisci presto e muto.
L'occasïone come viene scappa.
(a Mrs Quickly)
Chi vestirai da finta sposa?

QUICKLY
Un gaio ladron nasuto
Che abborre il Dottor Cajo.

MEG
(accorrendo dal fondo, ad Alice)
Ho nascosto i folletti lungo il fosso.
Siam pronte.

ALICE *(origliando)*
Zitto. Viene il **pezzo grosso**.

NANNETTA
Via!

ALICE
Via!

MEG
Via!

QUICKLY
Via!
*(Tutte fuggono con Fenton da sin-
istra.)*
*(Falstaff con due corna di cervo in
testa e avviluppato in un ampio man-
tello. Poi Alice. Poi Meg. Mentre
Falstaff entra in scena, suona la
mezzanotte.)*

FALSTAFF
Una, due, tre, quattro, cinque, sei,
sette botte,
Otto, nove, dieci, undici, dodici.
Mezzanotte.
(Vedendo la quercia di Herne)
Questa è la quercia. Numi,
proteggetemi! Giove!
Tu per amor d'Europa ti trasformasti
in bove;
Portasti corna. I numi c'insegnan la
modestia.
L'amore metamorfosa un uom in una
bestia.
*(Alice comparisce nel fondo. Falstaff
ascoltando.)*
Odo un soave passo!
Alice! Amor ti chiama!
(avvicinandosi ad Alice)
Vien! I'amor m'infiamma!

ALICE
(avvicinandosi a Falstaff)
Sir John!

FALSTAFF
Sei la mia damma!

ALICE
Sir John!

FALSTAFF
(afferrandola)
Sei la mia damma!

ALICE
O sfavillante amor!

FALSTAFF
(attirandola a sè con ardore)
Vieni! Già fremo e fervo!

ALICE
(sempre evitando l'abbraccio)
Sir John!

ANN

(*from faraway, coming nearer*)

Trust in the moon, love will always renew it!

FENTON

(*in the direction of where he heard Ann's voice*)

Yes, song will die on lips that are united.

ALICE

(*stepping between Ann and Fenton and forcing him to don the black hood*)

Just a moment! Put on this robe, and hurry!

(*Ann and Alice help Fenton to put on the robe. Quickly has appeared, wearing a huge bonnet and a grey coat. Her mask is that of an animal's snout.*)

FENTON

But what is this?

ANN

I'll tell you later.

ALICE

Don't worry!

ANN

(*looking at Fenton in disguise*)

He looks like one escaping from a convent.

ALICE

(*helping Fenton to don the mask*)

The wily ruse that my husband is planning, let us use it and turn it back upon him!

FENTON

A ruse, you say?

ALICE

Take my word! Be clever!
Obey me! The iron's hot . . .
we strike it now or never.

(*to Quickly*)

As bride-to-be whom have you chosen?

QUICKLY

That rogue with the big red nose
Who has raised the Doctor's dander.

MEG

(*entering from the rear, to Alice*)

All the children are hiding in the bushes. We're ready.

ALICE (*listening*)

Silence! Hear the happy hunter!

ANN

Hurry!

ALICE

Vanish!

MEG

Vanish!

QUICKLY

Hurry!

(*The women, together with Fenton, exeunt to the left*)

(*Falstaff, wearing an enormous pair of antlers and a wide coat, enters warily. During his entrance the midnight chimes are heard.*)

FALSTAFF

One, two, three, four, five, six, seven strokes . . .
Eight, nine, ten, eleven, twelve. It is midnight.

(*noticing Herne's Oak*)

Here is the oak tree. Mighty powers, stay with me!
Help me, Jove, who became a bull wearing horns for love of fair Europa.
I need your council.
The Gods teach us grace and resignation,
as love to humble beast will turn the glory of creation.

(*Alice appears in the rear. Falstaff listens.*)

Is this her tender footstep?
She's near me, drawn by my passion, . . .

(*goes towards her*)

. . . near me, for me to capture!

ALICE

(*approaching Falstaff*)

Sir John!

FALSTAFF

Show me compassion!

ALICE

Sir John!

FALSTAFF

Yield to my rapture!

ALICE

Oh blazing flame of love!

FALSTAFF

(*vainly trying to embrace her*)

Hear me . . . answer my craving!

ALICE

(*always avoiding his embraces*)

Sir John!

FALSTAFF

Sono il tuo servo!
Sono il tuo cervo imbizzarrito. Ed or
Piovan tartufi, rafani e finocchi!!!
E sien la mia pastura!
E amor trabocchi!
Siam soli . . .

ALICE

No. Qua nella selva densa mi segue
Meg.

FALSTAFF

È doppia l'avventura!
Venga anche lei! Squartatemi
Come un camoscio a mensa!!
Sbranatemi!!! Cupido
Alfin mi ricompensa
Io t'amo! t'amo!

MEG (di dentro)

Aiuto!!!

ALICE

(fingendo spavento)

Un grido! Ahimè!

MEG

(dal fondo, senza avanzare — non ha
la maschera)

Vien la tregenda!   (Fugge.)

ALICE

Ahimè! Fuggiamo!

FALSTAFF (spaventato)

Dove?

ALICE

(fuggendo da destra rapidissamente)

Il cielo perdoni al mio peccato!

FALSTAFF

(appiattandosi accanto al tronco della
quercia)

Il diavolo non vuol ch'io sia dannato.

NANNETTA (di dentro)

Ninfe! Elfi! Silfi! Doridi! Sirene!
L'astro degli incantesimi in cielo è
sorto.
Sorgete! Ombre serene!

(Comparisce nel fondo fra le fronde.

Falstaff gettandosi colla faccia contro
terra, lungo disteso.)

FALSTAFF

Sono le Fate. Chi le guarda è morto.

(Nannetta vestita da Regina delle Fate.
Alice: alcune Ragazzette vestite da
Fate bianche e da Fate azzurre. Falstaff sempre disteso contro terra, im-
mobile.)

ALICE

(sbucando cautamente da sinistra con
alcune Fate)

Inoltriam.

NANNETTA

(sbucando a sinistra con altre Fate e
scorgendo Falstaff)

Egli è là.

ALICE

(Scorge Falstaff e lo indica alle altre.)

Steso al suol.

NANNETTA

Lo confonde il terror.

(Tutte si inoltrano con precauzione.)

LE FATE

Si nasconde.

ALICE

Non ridiam!

LE FATE

Non ridiam!

NANNETTA

(indicando alle Fate il loro posto,
mentre Alice parte rapidamente da
sinistra)

Tutte qui, dietro a me. Cominciam.

LE FATE

Tocca a te.

(Le piccole Fate si dispongono in
cerchio intorno alla loro Regina: le
Fate più grandi formano gruppo a
sinistra.)

LA REGINA DELLE FATE

Sul fil d'un soffio etesio
Scorrete, agili larve;
Fra i rami un baglior cesio
D'alba lunare apparve.
Danzate! e il passo blando
Misuri un blando suon,
Le magiche accoppiando
Carole alla canzon,

LE FATE

La selva dorme e sperde
Incenso ed ombra; e par
Nell'aer denso un verde
Asilo in fondo al mar.

FALSTAFF

You are my doe and I am your stag,
  ranting and raving.
In a shower of truffles, radishes, and
  custard
the sky provide the supper
and love the mustard!
Alone here. . . .

ALICE

Wait! There in the wood behind us
is Mistress Page.

FALSTAFF

Good Fortune has combined us
all on one stage!
Now both of you, cut me in two! Divide
me!
Dismember me! Unto my altar you shall
  guide me!
I love you! I love you! I love you! . . .
  love you.

MEG (offstage)

Oh help me!

ALICE

(pretending to be frightened)

Good Heavens, a scream!

MEG

(appearing unmasked but staying in the
  shadow)

The host unholy! (flees)

ALICE

Alas! Let's flee them!

FALSTAFF (terrified)

Whereto?

ALICE

I pray to God for my salvation.

(runs off to the right)

FALSTAFF

(hiding near the oak-tree)

I never have a chance to court
damnation!

ANN (offstage)

Elfins! Fairies! Pixies! Spirits all, oh
  hear me!
Casting his magic spell on us, the moon
is smiling.
Arise now, shadows who cheer me!

(She has appeared among the trees.
  Falstaff, in panic, has thrown himself
  to the ground, face down.)

FALSTAFF

Unholy demons! No one lives who sees
them.

(Ann now is fully visible, disguised as
  Queen of the Fairies. A number of
  girls are dressed as white and as blue
  fairies. Falstaff remains on the
  ground, motionless.)

ALICE

(cautiously stepping forth with some of
  the fairies)

Follow me!

ANN

(cautiously advancing from the opposite side, noticing Falstaff)

There he lies.

ALICE

(noticing Falstaff also and pointing him
  out to the others)

. . . on the ground.

ANN

He is dying with fear.

(They all advance stealthily.)

FAIRIES

He is hiding.

ALICE

You be still!

FAIRIES

Yes, we will.

ANN

(instructing the fairies with regard to
  their actions, places, etc. while Alice
  exits rapidly to the left)

Do you know what to do?
Watch my cue!

FAIRIES

We're with you.

(A group of fairies form a circle
  around Ann. Another, taller group
  gathers to the left.)

QUEEN OF THE FAIRIES

Agleam in shimm'ring silverglow
And bathed in misty lather
Over the vale and hill below
Elves of the night forgather.
And gently, gently we sway
As we dance beneath the moon,
Smiling at him from faraway
We sing our haunting tune.

CHORUS OF ELVES

The forest slumbers without the slight-
est motion,
A world beneath an ocean,
A paradise below the sea.

LA REGINA DELLE FATE

Erriam sotto la luna
Scegliendo fior da fiore,
Ogni corolla in core
Porta la sua fortuna.
Coi gigli e le vïole
Scriviam de' nomi arcani,
Dalle fatate mani
Germoglino parole,
Parole alluminate
Di puro argento e d'or,
Carmi e malìe. Le Fate
Hanno per cifre i fior.

LE FATE
(mentre vanno cogliendo fiori)

Moviamo ad una ad una
Sotto il lunare albor,
Verso la quercia bruna
Del nero Cacciator.

(Tutte le Fate colla Regina mentre cantano si avviano lentamente verso la quercia.

Dal fondo a sinistra sbucano: Alice mascherata, Meg da Ninfa verde colla maschera, Mrs. Quickly da befana, mascherata. Sono precedute da Bardolfo, vestito con una cappa rossa, senza maschera, col cappucio abbassato sul volto e da Pistola, da satiro. Seguono: il Dr. Cajus, in cappa grigia, senza maschera, Fenton, in cappa nera, colla maschera, Ford, senza cappa nè maschera. Parecchi borghesi in costumi fantastici chiudono il corteggio e vanno a formare gruppo a destra. Nel fondo altri mascherati portano lanterne di varie fogge.)

BARDOLFO

Alto là!

(intoppando nel corpo di Falstaff e arrestando tutti con un gesto)

PISTOLA *(accorrendo)*

Chi va là?

FALSTAFF

Pietà!

QUICKLY
(toccando Falstaff col bastone)

C'è un uomo!

ALICE, MEG, E NANNETTA

C'è un uom!

LE FATE

Un uom!

FORD
(che sarà accorso vicino a Falstaff)

Cornuto come un bue!

PISTOLA

Rotondo come un pomo!

BARDOLFO

Grosso come una nave!

BARDOLFO, PISTOLA
(toccando Falstaff col piede)

Alzati, olà!

FALSTAFF
(alzando la testa)

Portatemi una grue! non posso.

FORD

È troppo grave.

QUICKLY

È corrotto!

LE FATE

È corrotto!

ALICE, NANNETTA E MEG

È impuro!

LE FATE

È impuro!

BARDOLFO
(con dei gran gesti da stregone)

Si faccia lo scongiuro!

ALICE
(in disparte a Nannetta, mentre il Dr. Cajus s'aggira come chi cerca qualcuno. Fenton e Quickly nascondono Nannetta colle loro persone.)

Evita il tuo periglio.
Già il Dottor Cajo ti cerca.

NANNETTA

Troviamo un nascondiglio.

QUICKLY

Poi tornerete lesti al mio richiamo.

(Nannetta, Fenton scompaiono dietro le fronde.)

BARDOLFO
(continuando i gesti di scongiuro sul corpo di Falstaff)

Spiritelli! Folletti!
Farfarelli! Vampiri! Agili insetti
Del palude infernale! Punzecchiatelo!
Orticheggiatelo!
Martirizzatelo
Coi grifi aguzzi!

(Accorrono velocissimi alcuni ragazzi vestiti da folletti, e si scagliano su Falstaff. Altri folletti, spiritelli, diavoli sbucano da varie parti. Alcuni scuotono crepitacoli, alcuni hanno in mano dei vimini; molti portano delle piccole lanterne rosse.)

QUEEN OF THE FAIRIES

The blossoms here and yonder,
Awakened by our dances,
View us with sleepy glances,
Rubbing their eyes in wonder.
The roses tell us a story
Of love and sweet surrender,
Lilies so proud and slender
Will sing of might and glory.
Trust in their magic powers,
Trust in their friendship true!
Knowing a secret, the flowers
Always confide it to you.

CHORUS OF ELVES

(*gathering flowers*)

Now slowly let us wander
There in the shadows blue
To the big oak tree yonder
Where we pay Herne his due.
(*During this chorus, all the Fairies
slowly approach the oak.*)

BARDOLPH

(*coming from upstage left, followed by
Alice in mask, Meg as the green
wood-nymph, Quickly as a witch, Dr.
Cajus in a grey cloak, not masked,
Pistol disguised as a satyr, Ford un-
disguised, Fenton in black robe and
mask. Several others wear phantastic
costumes, carrying lanterns of various
shapes and sizes.*)

What is this?
(*holding back the others as he comes
upon Falstaff's body*)

PISTOL (*joining Bardolph*)
Who goes there?

FALSTAFF
Alas!

QUICKLY
(*touching Falstaff with her broomstick*)
A human!

ALICE, MEG, ANN
A man!

FAIRIES
A man!

FORD
(*having come close to Falstaff*)
His horns bespeak defiance.

PISTOL
He must be born of giants.

BARDOLPH
Fit to serve on a platter.

BARDOLPH, PISTOL
(*kicking Falstaff*)
Up with you, arise!

FALSTAFF (*lifting his head*)
Without the help of science . . .
I cannot!

FORD
A weighty matter!

QUICKLY
He's a monster.

FAIRIES
He's a monster.

ALICE, ANN, MEG
What pollution!

FAIRIES
What pollution!

BARDOLPH
(*with gestures of a sorcerer*)
Let's plan his execution!

ALICE
(*aside to Ann while Dr. Cajus is looking
for someone. Fenton and Quickly are
hiding Ann.*)
Danger is near, be careful!
Our Doctor Cajus is snooping.

ANN
We'd better go in hiding.

QUICKLY
But come back here the moment I shall
call you!
(*Ann and Fenton disappear to the
rear.*)
BARDOLPH
(*standing over Falstaff's body, pretending to exorcise his spirit*)
Wicked servants of Satan! Ghouls and
goblins and demons!
Let us determine what to do with this
vermin!
Sap his sanity! Scratch at his vanity!
Hurt his humanity! Pluck him to
pieces!
(*A group of boys dressed as devils,
ghouls etc. come running from the
rear and pounce on Falstaff. Some of
them swing rattles and make noise in
other ways. Many of them carry little
red lamps.*)

FALSTAFF (*to Bardolph*)
I fear my fleece is shorn in profanity!

DEVILS, GOBLINS
(*tumbling Falstaff and rolling him over*)

Bundle him busily, Trundle him dizzily!
Jumble and rumble and tumble and humble him!
(*The goblins pinch and prick him.*)

ALICE, MEG, QUICKLY
Pricking and kicking torment him and trick him
For all his mendacity and his audacity!
Nick-to-the-quick him until you will lick him!

FALSTAFF
Oh! Oh! Oh! Oh!

DEVILS, GOBLINS
Deflate his propensity to shocking immensity!
His splendor so billowy turn slender and willowy!
The Master of Devilry shall lend you his lances,
The faster the revelry, the better the chances
To bite him and blight him, to smite and to spite him.
So pounce on him, hit him, and trounce him and twit him
Until in the end you completely defeat him!

ALICE, MEG, QUICKLY, FAIRIES
Tackle and shackle him, tatter and shatter him,
Knock him and rock him and sock him and batter him!
Prick him and tickle him for his audacity,
Pick-like-a-pickle him for his mendacity!
Fret and beset him for all his cupidity,
Make him regret his stupendous stupidity!
Prick him and nick him and kick him and tickle him!
(*Ford, Cajus, Pistol and Bardolph lift him up and force him to his knees!*)

DR. CAJUS, FORD
You loon!

BARDOLPH, PISTOL
Poltroon!

DR. CAJUS, FORD
Buffoon!

BARDOLPH, PISTOL
Balloon!

DR. CAJUS, FORD
Raccoon!

BARDOLPH, PISTOL
Baboon!

DR. CAJUS, BARDOLPH, FORD, PISTOL
You laughed too soon!!!

FORD
Treacherous gambler!

ALICE
Lecherous ambler!

BARDOLPH
Flasket-abuser!

QUICKLY
Basket-misuser!

PISTOL
Wonder-conniver!

MEG
Blundering diver!

DR. CAJUS
Paunchy rapscallion!

FORD
Haunchy old stallion!
(*Bardolph has taken Quickly's broomstick and is beating Falstaff.*)

BARDOLPH, PISTOL
Do you repent now?

FALSTAFF
I do repent now.

MEN
Can we relent now?
(*Bardolph again beating Falstaff*)

FALSTAFF
I do repent now.

MEN
Do you consent now?

FALSTAFF
I do repent now.

MEN
You loon! Poltroon! Buffoon!

FALSTAFF
I swoon.

FALSTAFF (*a Bardolfo*)
Ahimè! tu puzzi come una puzzola.

FOLLETTI E DIAVOLI
(*addosso a Falstaff spingendolo e fac-
endolo ruzzolare*)
Ruzzola, ruzzola,
Ruzzola, ruzzola!

ALICE, MEG, QUICKLY
Pizzica, pizzica,
Pizzica, stuzzica,
Spizzica, spizzica,
Pungi, spilluzzica,
Finch'egli abbài!

FALSTAFF
Ahi! Ahi! Ahi! Ahi!

FOLLETTI E DIAVOLI
Scrolliam crepitacoli,
Scarandole e nacchere!
Di schizzi e di zacchere
Quell'otre si macoli.
Meniam scorribandole,
Danziamo la tresca,
Treschiam le faràndole
Sull'ampia ventresca.
Zanzàre ed assilli,
Volate alla lizza
Coi dardi e gli spilli!
Ch'ei crepi di stizza!

ALICE, MEG E QUICKLY
Pizzica, pizzica,
Pizzica, stuzzica,
Spizzica, spizzica,
Pungi, spilluzzica
Finch'egli abbai!

ALICE, MEG, QUICKLY E FATE
Cozzalo, aizzalo
Dai pie' al cocuzzolo!
Strozzalo, strizzalo!
Gli svampi l'uzzolo!
Pizzica, pizzica, l'unghia rintuzzola!
Ruzzola, ruzzola, ruzzola, ruzzola!
(*Fanno ruzzolare Falstaff verso il pro-
scenio.*)

DR. CAJUS FORD
Cialtron!

BARDOLFO, PISTOLA
Poltron!

DR. CAJUS, FORD
Ghiotton!

BARDOLFO, PISTOLA
Pancion!

DR. CAJUS, FORD
Beòn!

BARDOLFO, PISTOLA
Briccon!

DR. CAJUS, FORD, BARDOLFO E PISTOLA
In ginocchion!

FORD
Pancia ritronfia!

ALICE
Guancia rigonfia!

BARDOLFO
Sconquassa-letti!

QUICKLY
Spacca-farsetti!

PISTOLA
Vuota-barili!

MEG
Sfonda-sedili!

DR. CAJUS
Sfianca-giumenti!

FORD
Triplice mento!

(*Bardolfo prende il bastone di Quickly
e dà una bastonata a Falstaff.*)

BARDOLFO, PISTOLA
Di' che ti penti!

FALSTAFF
Ahi! Ahi! mi pento!

TUTTI GLI UOMINI
Uom frodolento!

(*Bardolfo riprende il bastone e colpisce
nuovamente Falstaff.*)

FALSTAFF
Ahi! Ahi! mi pento!

GLI UOMINI
Uom turbolento!

FALSTAFF
Ahi! Ahi! mi pento!

GLI UOMINI
Capron! Scroccon! Spaccon!

FALSTAFF
Perdon!

BARDOLFO
(*colla faccia vicinissima alla faccia di
 Falstaff*)
Riforma la tua vita!

FALSTAFF
Tu puti d'acquavita.

LE DONNE
Domine fallo casto!

FALSTAFF
Ma salvagli l'addomine.

LE DONNE
Domine fallo guasto!

FALSTAFF
Ma salvagli l'addomine.

LE DONNE
Fallo punito Domine!

FALSTAFF
Ma salvagli l'addomine.

LE DONNE
Fallo pentito Domine!

FALSTAFF
Ma salvagli l'addomine.
DR. CAJUS, FORD, BARDOLFO E PISTOLA
Globo d'impurità! Rispondi.

FALSTAFF
Ben mi sta.
DR. CAJUS, FORD, BARDOLFO E PISTOLA
Monte d'obesità! Rispondi.

FALSTAFF
Ben mi sta.
DR. CAJUS, FORD, BARDOLFO E PISTOLA
Otre di malvasia! Rispondi.

FALSTAFF
Così sia.

BARDOLFO
Re dei panciuti!

FALSTAFF
Va via, tu puti.

BARDOLFO
Re dei cornuti!

FALSTAFF
Va via, tu puti.

TUTTI
Furfanteria!

FALSTAFF
Ahi! Così sia.

TUTTI
Gagliofferia!

FALSTAFF
Ahi! Così sia.

BARDOLFO
(*con veemenza*)
Ed or che il diavolo ti porti via!!!
(*Nella foga del dire gli casca il cap-
puccio.*)

FALSTAFF (*rialzandosi*)
Nitro! Catrame! Solfo!!!
Riconosco Bardolfo!

(*Violentissimamente contro Bardolfo*)

Naso vermiglio!
Naso bargiglio!
Puntùta lesina!
Vampa di resina!
Salamandra! Ignis fatuus! Vecchia
    alabarda! Stecca
Di sartore! Schidion d'inferno! **Aringa**
    secca!
Vampiro! Basilisco!
Manigoldo! Ladrone!
Ho detto. E se mentisco
Voglio che mi si spacchi il cinturone!!!

TUTTI
Bravo!

FALSTAFF
Un poco di pausa. Sono stanco.

QUICKLY
(*Che si trova vicino a Bardolfo, gli dice
 a bassa voce*)
Vieni. Ti coprirò col velo bianco.

FORD
Ed or, mentre vi passa la scalmana,
Sir John, dite: Il cornuto chi è?

ALICE, MEG
Chi è?

ALICE (*smascherandosi*)
Vi siete fatto muto?

FALSTAFF
(*dopo un primo istante di sbalordimento andando incontro a Ford*)
Caro signor Fontana!

BARDOLPH
(*coming close to Falstaff's face*)
You keep the Bible handy!

FALSTAFF
You rascal reek of brandy.

WOMEN
May the Almighty frighten him!

FALSTAFF
But never shrink or slighten him!

WOMEN
May the good Lord enlighten him!

FALSTAFF
But not reduce or tighten him!

WOMEN
Justice may put her bite on him.

FALSTAFF
Good Luck bestow her might on him!

WOMEN
Heaven may shed its light on him!

FALSTAFF
And Venus set her sight on him!

MEN
Mountain of mortal sin . . . your answer!

FALSTAFF
I agree.

MEN
Fountain of port and gin . . . your answer!

FALSTAFF
I agree.

MEN
Spout of deceit and outrage . . . your answer!

FALSTAFF
If you say so . . .

BARDOLPH
Lout let me warn you . . .

FALSTAFF
You reek of liquor . . .

BARDOLPH
I shall unhorn you!

FALSTAFF
. . . and make me sicker.

MEN
Watch how we beat you, . . .

FALSTAFF
Let me entreat you . . .

MEN
How we defeat you!

FALSTAFF
Let me entreat you!

BARDOLPH (*violently*)
. . . until the Devil will finally heat you.

(*His hood slides off his head.*)

FALSTAFF (*rising abruptly*)
Thunder and lightning! Satan!
This is Bardolph, so help me!

(*furiously assaulting Bardolph who re-
treats*)

Nose like a bunion,
Nose of a ronyon,
Bump of bibacity,
Lump of salacity!
Salamander! Blunted battle-ax! Fork of
the Devil!
Miserable mongrel! Infernal viper!
You scum incarnate! You bat, you gnat,
you rat!
You gallows-vulture! You varlet!
I have spoken. And if I am lying
No single bone of mine shall stay
unbroken!

ALL
Bravo!

FALSTAFF
Let's rest for a moment. I am tired.

QUICKLY
(*aside to Bardolph whom she then
draws behind the bushes*)
Come, it is time for you to be attired.

FORD
And now, while we shall all enjoy a
respite,
Sir John, tell me: Which of us wears
the horns?

ALICE, MEG
Say, who! Yes, who?

ALICE
(*taking off her mask*)
You seem confused and shaken.

FALSTAFF
(*reaching for Ford's hand*)
Good Master Brook, I greet you . . .

ALICE (*interponendosi*)
Sbagliate nel saluto,
Questo è Ford mio marito.

QUICKLY (*ritornando*)
Cavaliero,
Voi credeste due donne così grulle,
Così citrulle,
Da darsi anima e corpo all'Avversiero,
Per un uom vecchio, sùdicio ed
obeso . . .

MEG, QUICKLY
Con quella testa calva . . .

ALICE, MEG E QUICKLY
E con quel peso!!

FORD
Parlano chiaro.

FALSTAFF
Incomincio ad accorgermi
D'esser stato un somaro.

ALICE
Un cervo.

FORD
Un bue.

TUTTI (*ridendo*)
Ah! Ah!

FORD
E un mostro raro!

FALSTAFF
(*Che avrà riaquitata la sua calma*)
Ogni sorta di gente dozzinale
Mi beffa e se ne gloria;
Pur, senza me, costor con tanta boria
Non avrebbero un bricciolo di sale.
Son io che vi fa scaltri.
L'arguzia mia crea l'arguzia degli altri.

TUTTI
Ma bravo!

FORD
Per gli Dei!
Se non ridessi ti sconquasserei!
Ma basta. Ed or vo' che m'ascoltiate.
Coronerem la mascherata bella
Cogli sponsali della
Regina delle Fate.

(*Il Dr. Cajus e Bardolfo, vestito da Regina delle Fate col viso coperto da un velo, s'avanzano lentamente tenendosi per mano. Il Dr. Cajus ha la maschera sul volto.*)
Già s'avanza la coppia degli sposi.
È dessa!

TUTTI
Attenti!

FORD
Eccola in bianca vesta
Col velo e il serto delle rose in testa
E il fidanzato suo ch'io le disposi.
Circondatela, o Ninfe.

(*Il Dr. Cajus e Bardolfo si collocano nel mezzo: le Fate grandi e piccole il circondano.*)

ALICE
(*Presentando Nannetta e Fenton entrati da pochi istanti. Nannetta ha un gran velo celeste e fitto che la copre tutta. Fenton ha la maschera e la cappa.*)
Un'altra coppia
D'amanti desïosi
Chiede d'essere ammessa agli augurosi
Connubi!

FORD
E sia. Farem la festa doppia.
Avvicinate i lumi. Il ciel v'accoppia.

(*I folletti guidati da Alice si avvicinano colle loro lanterne. Alice prenderà in braccio il più piccolo dei ragazzetti che sarà mascherato da spiritello, e farà in modo che la lanterna che tiene in mano illumini in pieno la faccia di Bardolfo appena questi reserà senza il velo che lo nasconde. Un altro spiritello guidato da Meg illuminerà Nannetta e Fenton.*)
Giù le maschere e i veli. Apoteòsi!

(*Al commando di Ford rapidamente Fenton e il Dr. Cajus si tolgono la maschera. Nannetta si toglie il velo e Quickly toglie il velo a Bardolfo: tutti rimangono a viso scoperto.*)

TUTTI
Ah! Ah! Ah! Ah!

DR. CAJUS
(*riconscendo Bardolfo, immobilizzato dalla sorpresa*)
Spavento!

FORD (*sorpreso*)
Tradimento!

ALICE (*interrupting him*)

I fear you are mistaken . . .

This is Ford, my good husband.

QUICKLY (*returning*)

I am honored!

So you fancied two ladies, choosing
   freely, could be so silly
and court, body and soul, their own
   perdition
for some old charmer clearly out of
   season . . .

QUICKLY, MEG

. . . whose vanity and fat have . . .

QUICKLY, MEG, ALICE

. . . clouded his reason?

FORD

Now you know it!

FALSTAFF

I begin to perceive that likely
I shall have been made an ass.

ALICE

A roebuck!

FORD

A bullock!

ALL (*laughing*)

Ha, ha, ha!

FORD

. . . a curious monster, a funny freak!

FALSTAFF

(*having regained his composure*)

Thus a rabble of commonplace barbar-
   ians derides me,
Gloating in glory!
Yet, but for me, this dull and witless
   story
Would not even have a pinch of salt
   to spice it!
'Tis I, yes, I alone, noble and clever,
Whose gay adventure you will remem-
   ber forever!

WOMEN

Well spoken!

FORD

Be it said that, had I not had fun, you
   would be dead!
Enough now! There are more impor-
   tant matters:
Before this gay, enchanted night is
   ended
A royal wedding-feast now bids fair to
   be attended!

(*Dr. Cajus and Bardolph, disguised as
Queen of the Fairies, advance slowly,
holding hands. Bardolph's face is
hidden by his veil while Dr. Cajus
wears a mask.*)

See the couple approaching from the
   distance.

Behold them!

FALSTAFF, CHORUS

Behold them!

FORD

Ravishing, so fair and slender,
The lovely bride all garbed in silv'ry
   splendor!
He, manly, strong and handsome, cho-
   sen with my assistance.
Let the elfins surround them.

(*Bardolph and Dr. Cajus arrive center-
stage, surrounded by Fairies.*)

ALICE

(*presenting Ann and Fenton. Ann is
covered by a long blue veil, Fenton
still wears his monk's robe.*)

Another pair of young hearts in sweet
   communion
Came here, fervently hoping that you
   would sanction their union.

FORD

How charming! We heartily invite
   them!
Bring on the lights and lanterns! May
   Heav'n unite them!

(*Led by Alice, a group of goblins come
forward, carrying lanterns. The
smallest one, carried by Alice, holds
his tiny lantern on a level with Bardolph's face. Ann and Fenton, hand
in hand, are standing slightly off
center-stage.*)

Now remove your disguises! Apotheosis!

(*As soon as they hear Ford's command,
Cajus and Fenton drop their masks.
Ann unveils her face, and Quickly
pulls the hood off Bardolph's head.
All the faces are uncovered.*)

ALL except FORD and CAJUS

Ha, ha, ha, ha!

DR. CAJUS (*recognizing Bardolph*)

Oh terror!

FORD (*thunderstruck*)

What an error!

GLI ALTRI
(*ridendo*)

Apoteòsi!

FORD
(*guardando l'altra coppia*)

Fenton con mia figlia!!!

DR. CAJUS

Ho sposato Bardolfo!! Spavento!

TUTTI

Evviva! Evviva!

FORD
(*ancora sotto il colpo dello stupore*)

Oh! meraviglia!

ALICE

L'uom cade spesso nelle reti ordite
Dalle malizie sue.

FALSTAFF
(*avvicinandosi a Ford con un inchino
ironico*)

Caro buon Messer Ford, ed ora, dite:
Lo scornato chi è?

FORD
(*accenna al Dr. Cajus*)

Lui.

DR. CAJUS
(*accenna a Ford*)

Tu.

FORD

No.

DR. CAJUS

Sì

FENTON
(*accenna pure al Dr. Cajus e Ford*)

Lor.

DR. CAJUS
(*mettendosi con Ford*)

Noi.

FALSTAFF

Tutti e due.

ALICE
(*mettendo Falstaff con Ford e il Dr.
Cajus*)

No. Tutti e tre.

(*a Ford, mostrando Nannetta e Fenton*)

Volgiti e mira quelle ansie leggiadre.

NANNETTA
(*a Ford giungendo le mani*)

Perdonateci, padre.

FORD

Chi schivare non può la propria noia
L'accetti di buon grado.
Facciamo il parentado
E che il ciel vi dia gioia.

TUTTI

Evviva!

FALSTAFF

Un coro e terminiam la scena.

FORD

Poi con Sir Falstaff, tutti, andiamo a
cena.

TUTTI

Evviva!

FUGA

Tutto nel mondo è burla.
L'uom è nato burlone,
La fede in cor gli ciurla,
Gli ciurla la ragione.
Tutti gabbati! Irride
L'un l'altro ogni mortal.
Ma ride ben chi ride
La risata final.

CALA LA TELA

FALSTAFF, CHORUS

Apotheosis!

FORD

(*noticing the other couple*)

Fenton with my daughter!

DR. CAJUS

I am married to Bardolph! Oh terror!

WOMEN

Be happy! Be happy!

FORD

(*still in a state of shock*)

I cannot grasp it.

ALICE

The finest web our perfidy can fashion
will often trap the weaver!

FALSTAFF

(*walking up to Ford and bowing, with
irony*)

Ah, my good Master Ford, I pray you
tell me which of us is the fool!

FORD

(*pointing to Dr. Cajus*)

He.

DR. CAJUS

(*pointing to Ford*)

You.

FORD

No.

DR. CAJUS

Yes.

FENTON

(*indicating both Ford and Dr. Cajus*)

Both.

DR. CAJUS

(*stepping close to Ford*)

We.

FALSTAFF

There are two now!

ALICE

No!

(*pointing to Falstaff, Ford and Dr.
Cajus*)

There are three!

(*to Ford, referring to Ann and Fenton*)

Look on the children on pins and
needles!

ANN

(*entreating Ford with hands folded*)

Dearest Father, forgive us!

FORD

When you suffer defeat, don't let it
blight you:
It never shall disgrace you!
My children, I embrace you!
Let me bless and unite you!

ALL

Be happy!

FALSTAFF

A rousing tribute to the winner!

FORD

Then with Sir John I ask you all to
dinner.

ALL

We thank you!

FUGUE

Let us enjoy our folly!
Man is born to be jolly!
His idle pretenses, vain defences
Trouble his senses, confound his mind.
Leaner or fatter we frolic and flatter,
Let us be merry and let us pretend:
Fun is the triumph of mind over matter
If we laugh in the end!

END OF OPERA